The Circumpunct
A Symbol of God and Gold

Holly S. Remkes

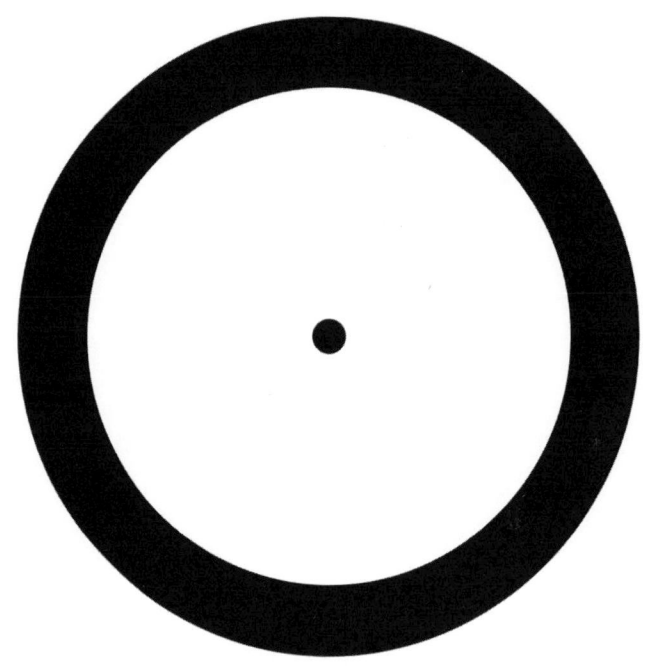

A Study of Treasure Symbols

Book 1

Copyright © Holly S. Remkes.
All rights reserved. No part of this book may be reproduced or used in any manner without written consent.

ISBN: 9798665579115

Introduction

Holly S. Remkes

    I hope this simple little book will help the desert detective in deciphering what is written or hidden in stone at important sites where things of value are contained.

  I hope the information I share will help the prospector find the mineral veins and old mines that are marked out by the ancients and old timers for future generations. I hope to share information that will help archeologists and historians. I hope to shed light on what has been cloaked and hidden in a veil of symbols. I hope to share information that will unlock doors to the mysteries and wisdom of the ages.

    I hope that you may more fully understand yourself and God, and find hidden treasures as you become more aware of the knowledge and hidden language veiled in layers of symbols and meanings.

This book contains my thoughts and ideas, and information that I have gathered on my journey to gain understanding. Much of the information is from what I have read on the internet, or gleaned from books as I have done extensive research trying to make sense of what I was seeing. The conclusions I have come up with reflect where I am in my research and understanding of things at this point in time, but may change as I grow and study more. I hope that you can take what I am sharing and use it for good.

The photos in this book of rocks, and writings, and mountains were taken by me while exploring Utah. Most of the photos I used to illustrate ideas were ones that I took, or created but there were a few, that were taken from the Public Domain and then edited.

Acknowledgements

A thank you to my sister, Stephanie, for the butterfly pictures, and to Dane Horrocks for the picture of the pretty Chrysanthemums, to LauraLee Anderson for the picture of her family roasting marshmallows around the fire, to Sarah Skeem for the picture of my Dad's assay bead and his counterfeit silver. A thank you to the Beckwith family for letting me use Frank's photo of the Fillmore Mysteryglyphs.
I would like to thank all of my family and friends, those

who have been with me from the begining and to those who have walked the path with me for a season or two. And for those new friends that I meet on a daily basis.
I would like to thank my family and kids for all of the fun adventures and for listening to me as I try to decipher what I am seeing at sites. And, "Thank you" to my husband, David, for letting me bounce ideas back and forth with him at all hours of the night.
I would like to thank my daughter, Acacia for her drawing of the solar system.
I would like to thank Stefan Duncan for letting me share some of his beautiful artwork.
 A big thank you to my sister Jeana and her family for the adventures we shared while her youngest was still little enough that she had to be carried.
 And a huge, "Thank you" to my brother Nathan for always being ready to go on an adventure at the spur of the moment, and for all of the awesome and crazy things that we have seen together. You are the only one who knows which site and location I am referring to when I say "The Isaac Site" or "Dad's Cave" or "King's Fifth" or the "Seal Site" or even specifics like the "Skull near Chief Chinko."
A thank you to those on my family tree. To my parents and grandparents, and to the countless others who have helped shape me. I have been blessed to have walked in some of the same places as my ancestors, and to have

spent time pondering at many of the same locations.
A thank you, to great-grandpa Stanley and his father and his father's father who left behind a story in our geneology that triggered a desire to know more about their mines. And a special Thank You, to great-great-great grandpa Augustus, whose writings left in Southern Utah might be considered as Native American Rock Art to those who only see the art without looking deeper.

●

The tiny speck of awareness, a little dot of thought, a tiny seed of faith or fear, of love or hate, or of things imagined, all can grow into something much more. A speck of curiousity can grow into a fuller understanding of things if properly persued.

As a child, I explored the desert with my family. I started noticing things that didn't make sense to me. The writings on the rocks, or petroglyphs were always somewhat of a curiosity to me but I was told they were

just art or the works of a Native American Shaman who had ingested psychedelic mushrooms, or drawings done by Native tribes who were writing about their hunting trips. I was told from many sources and experts that the writings, if there was even any meaning, could only be understood by those who wrote them and that it was disrespectful to try to understand things, especially since I was not a Native American. At one location where some petroglyphs were fenced off, the BLM erected a sign that stated, "Petroglyphs are an ancient Indian rock art from before 1000 A.D. The meaning if any, is unknown but some authorities think these symbols were an agreement dividing water and hunting rights among the Indians..." Say what?
Signs like this, almost closed my curiosity to the point that I almost belived it wasn't worth even thinking about the things that were written.

  I also noticed other types of writings at many of these locations. Often, it appeared there were many different time frames when things had been written. Some looked quite recent, and I was told it was all graffiti and vandalism. Then I started noticing there was something strange about the rocks at a lot of these locations.

  During my childhood years, I would spend time

out prospecting with my dad, and doing all types of camping and rockhounding trips. I remember my dad pointing out unusual things. "That mountain looks like an eagle," or "that mountain sure looks like a pyramid."

I married and had children and didn't get out to the desert very often. But the mysteries of the desert were there at the back of my mind for those many years of taking care of my babies and trying to help my husband with his ambitions.

When my youngest son was still a toddler, one of my sisters came across a story of a treasure that was hid by a man named Forrest Fenn. He had a poem that was on the internet that mentioned clues to where he hid his treasure. We were convinced it was somewhere in Yellowstone and were wanting to go and look for it. However, we had families and the time and expense to go on such and adventure wasn't going to work as I had 7 kids still at home and my sister also had a lot of family responsiblities as well.

We started researching treasure stories closer to home and came across the story of Herschal Hill and his grain gold hidden somewhere in a cave perhaps in the Cricket mountains. We were convinced we could find this treasure as the story we read seemed to describe the area pretty well. However, we were soon to learn there were many versions of this story and the descriptions were all different. We also discovered, just how big the desert really was when you are looking for a spot big enough to climb into.

During this time, some of my other siblings became involved a little, and we started exploring other possible locations. We also started taking photographs of strange things we were noticing out in the desert and realized there was a lot more history than we were aware of.

We bought books. Lots of books. Books on treasure symbols, and Spanish markers and monuments. One set of books by Charles Kenworthy stuck out the most. The information he spoke of seemed preposterous. Some of the markers he described made absolutely no sense to me, and I concluded that he was out of touch with reality. My first reaction after reading his books were that I should throw them away. Except... except that I had seen some of the markers he had mentioned. And they made absolutey no sense to me. A mountain that looked like a face. That is a little weird to think something like that could be tied to a cache site. Nature does some really cool things. But... what if?
No way... but... hmmm...

Somewhere during this time, I came across a story in my family history about some mines my great-grandpa loved and worked, but lost because he wasn't able to get the assesment work done on time, and a neighbor from the nearby town legally claimed over them. I had a burning desire to find these mines, and so I had another area that I started to explore and to find strange things that began more questions.

    I started to see. And after seeing, I could see a little bit more. I started backing up and really looking. I started to pay attention more to the things that didn't make sense. I started reaching out to people who might know something on the topic that I had just become aware of. I started to understand a tiny speck and a tiny speck more. Perhaps this is part of the illumination process, or the faith process. The more we see, the more we can see.

    I started researching and cataloging what I was seeing. I soon realized that I lived in the perfect time of history to find the answers to a lot of these hidden things without having to belong to any secret society or any particular group or organization. The age of information has made finding answers easier.

    The things I began to see sometimes confused me. Were these things good or bad? Were the people who made these markers and who hid these things up good or bad? I realized early on that any time you are dealing with wealth and knowledge, you will likely have both. And most of the time, even with a symbol, it can be used for both the good and the bad.

Symbols are some of the best ways to hide important information in plain sight. The language of symbols is rich and can say so much more than most any other type of writing.

A symbol can mean something totally different to different people, so it is important to understand the context or the ideas of the people who may have shared what is written.

Symbols often have layered meanings. Many times, all of the meanings are accurate, but the deeper the layer, the more likely there is valuable information to be found.

For instance, look at the goat symbol found written on the rocks in almost all areas of the world. Most people do not question why the goat, ram or ibex symbol is found worldwide. Some will say it is just art, others will say the Natives liked drawing pictures depicting their hunting. Some of the goats are pretty funny looking with two heads, or extra legs. Some have odd shaped bodies or horns coming out of their backs.

Most people, Natives included, have no clue as to what a lot of the petroglyphs are. There are some who understand, at least to some degree, and by studying these people and the symbols themselves, I believe many of the writings can be understood.

I definitely don't have all of the answers, but I believe that if the messages were left for someone with an understanding of these symbols, then these types of messages can be decoded.

Often times, I believe, the intended meaning will often have to be looked at through a larger scope than just a lone symbol. Such as the letters in the alphabet. The letter I can be mean "I" but if it is used with other letters and arrangements, it may spell out a totally different idea. Often, symbols are mixed with others for added meanings. It is wise to look at all of the information to determine the context of the what the symbol may represent. Sometimes, the symbols that are written are used to catch your attention, so you can see what is hidden in stone.

I hope that this book will help you see more. And I hope you gain more perspective. I hope to share some of the rocks I have seen, and some of the writings I have studied as I have done extensive research as a desert detective.

At first, I wasn't sure where to start with this project of sharing this information. But it became apparent that I should start with the simplest symbol, and so that is what this first book is about, THE CIRCUMPUNCT.

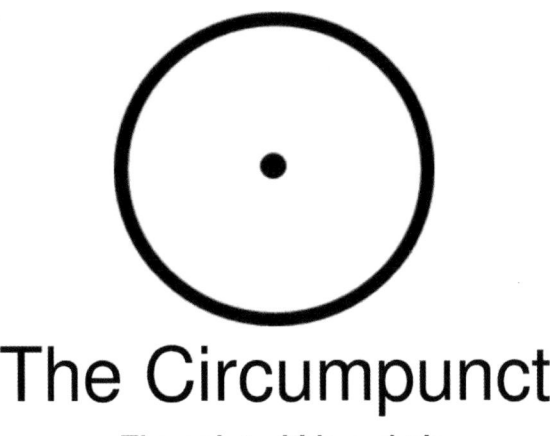

The Circumpunct

-The point within a circle-
-The point within a point-

The circumpunct is one of the oldest symbols known to man. There are many layers of meaning in this symbol. The dot can remind us of the point of the beginning of creation. The dot is one of the most primitive and fundamental symbols and is like the beginning of anything. It is the "I am" to look within ourselves to find order.

"**Ante omnia Punctum exstitit…**"
"**Before all things were, there was a point.**" Anonymous, 18th century 'Le Mystere de la Croix'

The word "circumpunct" **appears to come from the Latin prefix** "CIRCUM" **meaing: around or round, and the suffix** "PUNCT" **which is also Latin and means, point, prick or pierce.**

When the dot is surrounded by a circle, it reminds us of expansion. It can also remind us that something is contained within.
It is the symbol for gold and God and the sun.

The Seed.
Expansion and Growth.
If you look to nature, you may begin to understand this symbol.

Garden of the Heart

In a garden near are growing
Seedlings that the eye can't see.
In a day, of when not knowing,
Those seeds will grow and show through me.

Inside my heart the fertile land,
So many things may flourish.
Seeds will sprout beneath this sand
And will grow if only nourished.

I'm the garnder of my heart!
I'm in charge of what I grow!
Doubt and fear will gain no start -
For I'm in charge of what I grow.

Seeds of hate and envy – Never!
Forgiveness, love, faith, and courage,
Sweet fruits of these go on forever
Procrastination I discourage.

I'll plant the seeds of greatness in me
With vision to see them multiplied.
In the day of harvest, greatly
I'll see well what I have tried.

The seeds which yield a worthy share
Are such priceless seeds indeed.
But they will need more tender care
Than a free-willed growing weed.

So plant your garden carefully
Worthless thoughts pluck away.
Nourish seeds of greatness – Ere for we -
We shall reap on harvest day!

Under the right conditions a seed will expand and grow and will produce more of its kind multiplied. The law of the harvest is evident in the world around us. What we sow we will reap, and usually more than what we have sown. When a kernal of corn is planted, an entire cob of corn is expected at harvest time. We generally know not to anticipate a harvest in the same season we sow. Sometimes, though, I personally have to remember this principle when I am working on improving a difficult relationship or am trying to better my situations. Sometimes, even with my physical or spiritul betterment I am wanting instant results.

4

In some ancient South-Slavic Languages the tree ring is called "God" and the word for a year is called "Godiva."

If fertilized, and under the right conditions, an egg has the potential to grow.

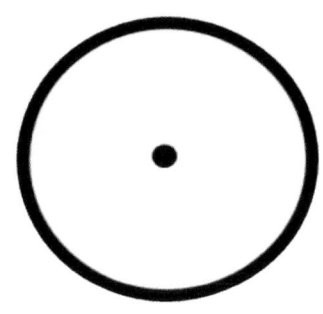

The beginning of existence.

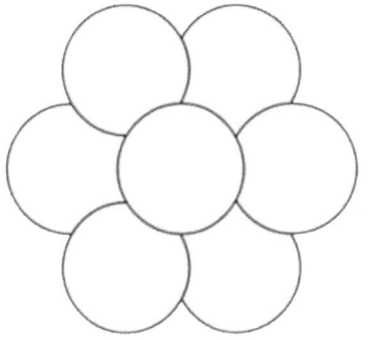

The egg of life.

The seed of life.

The flower of life.

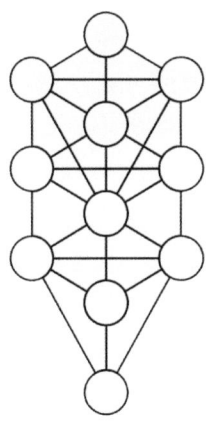

The tree of life.

The sun is the center of our solar system.

The closer to the center or the point of origin will be the strongest, as is shown in this ripple. I like to use this principle in my life.

The closer we stand to the fire will be the warmest. And the refiner's fire can be purifying.

The closer we can get to the origin of information the more accurate the information will be. The closer we can get to God, the more light and understanding we will have to help us with our own lives. If we can get our information from God instead of the world, we will have the ability to have the more accurate way to live a life filled with happiness and success.

This life is the time for us to prepare to meet our Creator, who is our Father in Heaven. When Adam and Eve partook of the fruit of the Tree of Knowledge of Good and Evil, they were cut off from the presence of God both physcially and spiritually. God set up cherubim to keep them from partaking of the Tree of Life and living forever in an unclean state. And as no unclean thing can stand in the presence of God, we would require a refining process to become clean again through the atonement of Christ. Our Savior Jesus Christ was prepared from before the foundation of the world to help us return back to live in the presence of God. And through Him we would be able to live both physcially and spiritually. He is the only way. Christ is the Word which in the begining was God. He helped the Father create this world in which we live. Christ is our connection to heaven. And I believe, that as children of God we have the ability to become like God through His only begotten Son.

Sometimes it may be tempting to believe that God does not exist because there are so many terrible things that can happen in this mortal life. And if He did exist, why wouldn't He come and take away pain and hurt and all the sad and horrible things. I believe that we need to be purified. I also believe that God can see the big picture, and I often have to remind myself to trust that this life is only a small point in the eternity of things. God is bigger and better than what we may be going through. His perspective is eternal. And we needed this mortal existence to help us to become like our Eternal Father.

****

A Random Thought on Sun Poop

In my research I came across some information that I thought was funny. The word Teocuitlatl is the Nahuatl term for gold, and according to some sources Teocuitlatl means "excrement of the Gods."

In Florentine Codex, book 11 on Earthy Things (originally written in the 16th century) it mentions that gold is "god's excrement" and that it looks "something like a little bit of diarrhea." However, when I researched the etymology on the word "excrement" it goes to the Latin word "excernere" which means "to sift out." This meaning reminds me of the sifting out or refining process to gain pure gold, or the sifting out, such as panning for gold.

Purified Gold

Faith is a purifying and refining process.

I wonder if the story found in Daniel Chapter 3 of the Bible, of Shadrach, Meshach, and Abendego could be an example of symbolically becoming so close to God that these men were not consumed during their firey trial. Not only were they refined enough to stand in the fire without being consumed, but the Son of God was with them. True faith will purify us and will help us become closer to God. These men knew that God could deliver them from the firery furnace. " But if not..." They also had the faith, and acted according to that faith.

The word "Mediator" is from Latin, and is from the word "Medio" which means to "be in the middle." The word "medius" is also Latin and means "middle."

> "I would that ye should look to the Great Mediator, and hearken unto his great commandments." 2 Nephi 2:28

13

According to one definition in the dictionary "Mediator means " a person who attempts to make people involved in a conflict come to an agreement; a go-between."

Christ is known as the "Great Mediator." He is the mediator between us and the Father. He didn't make up the difference where we fall short, but He is the difference. The law was appeased and through Christ, justice and mercy could both be satisfied.

We were able to come to this mortal existence and learn and grow and make mistakes because we chose to follow Christ's plan that was laid down before the world was created. It is said in scripture that 1/3 of the Hosts of Heaven chose not to follow Christ in the prexistence. The others chose to follow Lucifer. He had became fallen. He wanted to make us all be good without making mistakes. He also wanted to take all the glory for himself. We can still see his influence in the way some people and governments want to take away free agency and make everyone safe.

Lucifer's name means "Morning Star" or "Light bearer." But we must remember that Lucifer fell and is no longer light. His ways are not light.

Christ is also refered to in scripture as the "Morning Star." This can be confusing to some, and many people find themselves associated with things they find abhorent, as they thought they were following illumination and light, only to find out they were deceived and the path they were following was, "anything BUT light."

This has happend thought the ages, through almost all religions and in all countries. From the beginning, Satan began counterfeiting truth. Cain and later Lamech (with the guidance of Lucifer) took and counterfeited many of the truths that were taught to Adam. You can see this as you study many cultures. Instead of a sacrifice of a broken heart, and a contrite spirit, to the Son of God-- a beating human heart and human sacrifice given to a Sun god. The list of the many corruptions and atrocities is long. Even the Christian religion has not been spared the deception that has harmed many, even supposedly in the very the name of Christ. But the root of most of these evil practices has been the lucre and power, and a never satisfying desire to fill an ever taking void of the dissatisfaction of chasing carnal cravings. It is my belief that we all have an quiet inner guide that can help us, not only from being decieved but it can also help us back onto the right path if we have been led astray.

The account of creation found in Genesis says:

In the beginning God created the heavens and the earth. And the earth was without form, and void; and darkness was upon the face of the deep. And the Spirit of God moved upon the face of the waters. And God said, Let there be light: and there was light. And God saw the light, that it was good: and God divided the light from the darkness. And God called the light Day, and the darkness he called Night. And the evening and the morning were the first day.

The Sunflower

The evidence of the hand of God can be found in nature. As I studied what many of the experts had to say on the topic of the symbol of the sun, many of them concluded that Christ is not real. My thoughts from studying the same symbol, only gave me a stronger testimony of the divinity and the nature of Christ.

I love the passage found in Alma 30 of The Book of Mormon where Alma speaks to Korihor, the Anti-Christ. Alma says:
"The scriptures are laid before thee, yea, and all things denote there is a God; yea, even the earth, and all things that are upon the face of it, yea, and its motion, yea, and also all the planets which move in their regular form do witness that there is a Supreme Creator."

The Chrysanthemum Seal
The Imperial Seal of Japan
菊紋, Kikumon

The Chrysanthemum

According to online sources, the Chrysanthemum (originally denoting the corn marigold) is from Latin, which is from the Greek word Khrusanthemon or "gold flower" from Khurs-khruso-chryso and anthemon which is flower.

Ars Magna Lucis et Umbrae
The Great Art of Light and Shadow
(By Jesuit scholar Athanasius Kircher 1646)

Ars Magna Lucis et Umbrae

"The title in Latin, was intended as a play on words. "We say 'Magna' on account of a kind of hidden allusion to the magnet," Kircher wrote in his introductory pages. So the title could also be read as "The Magnetic Art of Light and Shadow."

Kircher's works were about magnetism, optics, treating light, shadow, refraction, projection, distortion and luminescence. He had many early descriptions of the camera obscura and magic lantern. I find this interesting because John Gutzon de la Mothe Borglum, the American sculptor known for Mt. Rushmore, and associated with Stone Mountain, created a gigantic magic lantern to project the image of a model of the carving onto the side of the mountain, which helped him greatly in his massive sculpture.

***

When I first looked at this work of art, I thought it was portraying how Satan counterfeits. How he uses light to reflect and appear to have his own light. However, I am not certain that this was the intended meaning being portayed in this illustration. But, seeing how these people tend to put layered meanings in their works, I am not going to dismiss this possibility. There is a lot to learn from this image, in relations to how vault and cache sites are hid up. They use light and shadow to hide information. They also used methods to shape the rocks at these sites that were meant to look natural. And some of the works are very massive.

The opposing factors and deception are also a huge part of the way many of the sites containing things of value are set up.

Counterfeit Silver Coins

My dad was disappointed with his purchase after testing these coins, as they definitely were not silver.

Unfortunately, whenever there is anything of value, as in truth, knowledge, beauty or wealth, there will always be found a counterfeit. These counterfeits often confuse people.

According to wikipedia: To counterfeit means to imitate something authentic, with the intent to steal, destroy, or replace the original, for use in illegal transactions, or otherwise to deceive individuals into believing that the fake is of equal or greater value than the real thing.

In my years of doing a scrap gold business, I have run into many counterfeits. I would mainly buy gold jewelry items. It seems the heavier, or more valuable the item, the more likely there will be a counterfeit. Many of the religious items, and men's chains fall into this category.

14K gold ring -------------- Fake gold chain

    I have learned how to spot most counterfeits. I also have a good acid testing kit. A counterfeit will generally be extra shiny, and on chains and neckaces, won't have the right markings done on the tiny part of the clasps, but will often be marked with the 14k or gold marks in a very obvious and misleading way. If I can hold the item, it will usually feel wrong. Gold generally has a nice weight, and also has an attractive feel to it, while a counterfeit will not feel right. It will not hold up under the acid test, and it certainly won't hold up if put into the refiner's furnace.

Real gold being weighed to calculate the value based on the purity level.

Real holds up---------------------- Fake dissolves

Clasp of a common counterfeit gold chain

Clasp of a real, common style, 14k gold chain
Notice the 14k marked on the tiny part of the clasp on a real chain. (Sometimes, a real chain may have been repaired with a fake clasp and sometimes there might be a real clasp on a fake chain, so it is good to test anything suspicious.)

In God We Trust

Many things in our society aren't what they may appear. I have always liked the saying "In God We Trust" and appreciate it being on the American currency. However, I believe it may have a sinister reversal in meaning on our currency today. It does not state in which God we trust. Most of the money in the US at this time, is not backed by anything of value. The Federal Reserve Bank created nothing out of thin air. Our current fiat money is not backed by anything but debt. Gold and silver currency is a much more honest and safe currency as it has something to back it. Our belief and faith in the fiat money is the main thing that keeps it working. If ever our belief in it falls, it will fall.
In fact, the origin of the word "Fiat" is from Latin meaning, "let it be done." This first appears in Genesis in the Latin translation of the Bible. "Fiat Lux" or "Let there be light."
It seems the creators of the fiat money literally created something out of nothing, or accomplished a perverted version of the Philosopher's Stone. They created the essence of wealth or of fake gold out of thin air. It is an illusion, and in my mind a counterfeit of what real wealth should be. It has literally created a nation of slavery.

Other counterfeits we should watch for are all around us and do the opposite of the true thing of value. Usually these things will be tied to the carnal side of our physical existence, such as the search for happiness in the external and carnal world without having the balance of an inner substance.

From running a scrap gold business, I have come to learn and appreciate that there is a core value to precious metals.
Even when a gold chain is broken, it still holds the same core value in weight as a wearable chain. It might not be as pretty or as useful, but it still holds its base value. I believe that we, as children of God, all have the same value, whether we are broken, dirty or damaged.

Jesus Christ, The Son of God

Christ in Greek is: Χριστός
  Christós

Etymology on the word Christ comes from the Greek word χριστός (Chrīstós) which means "anointed one." The word is derived from the Greek verb χρίω (chrī́ō), which means "to anoint."

Gold in ancient Greek is: χρῡσός
  khrūsós
  Chrysus
  Khrysos

In Greek mythology Chrysus is the spirit of gold.
In Greek, the word κρίσις (Crisis) means a decisive point.

Monarch Butterfly Chrysalis

Chrysalis is a Latin word which comes from Ancient Greek χρυσαλλίς khrysallis, which means "golden **pupa** of the butterfly," from khrysos, "gold."

30

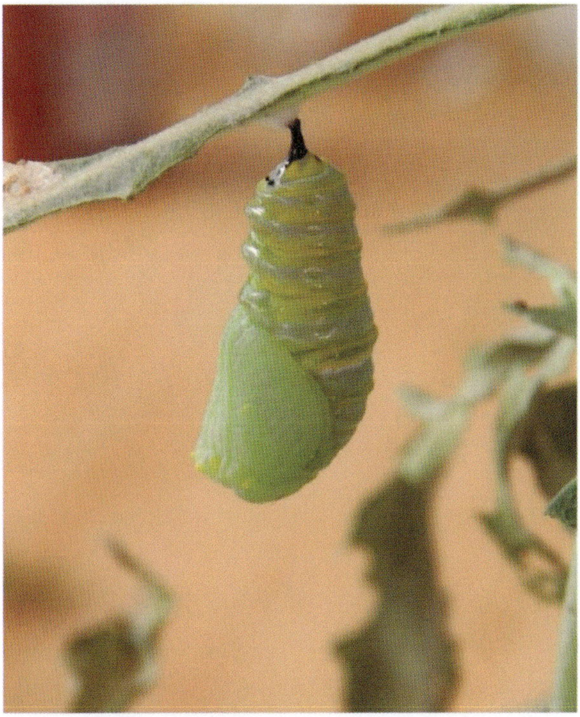

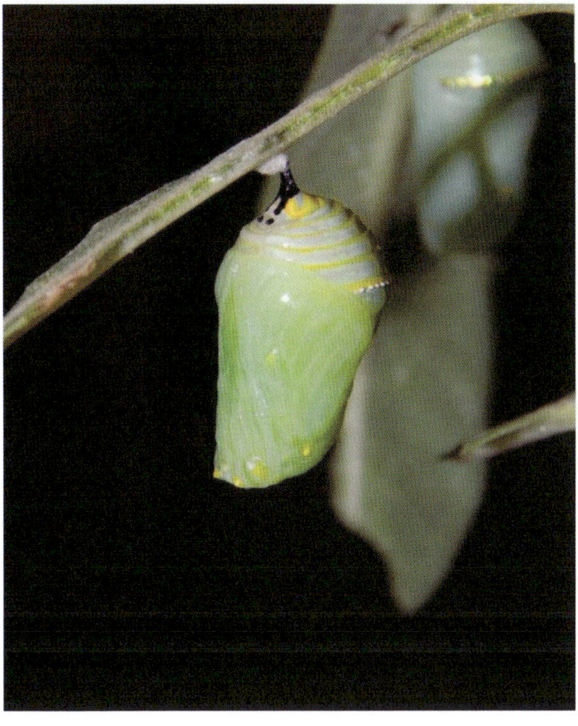

(Unenhanced Photo)

(Photo Enhanced)

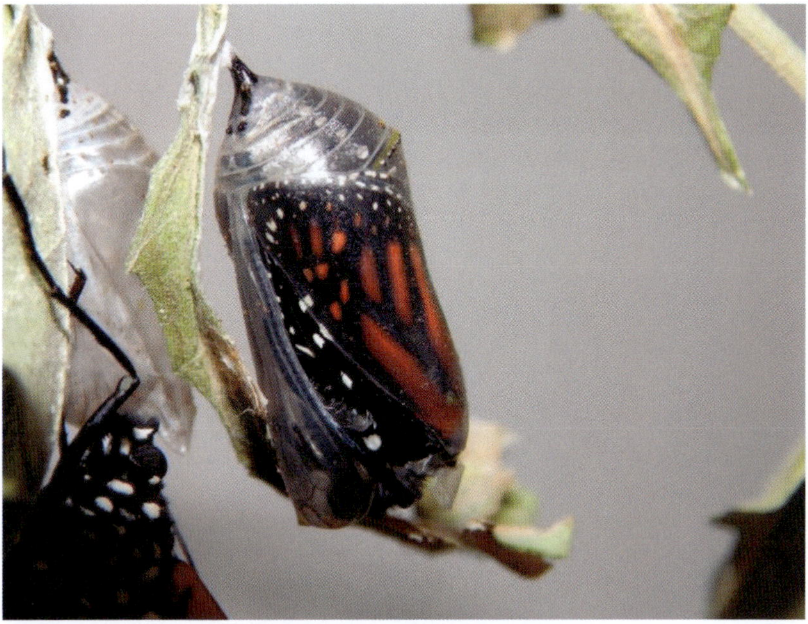

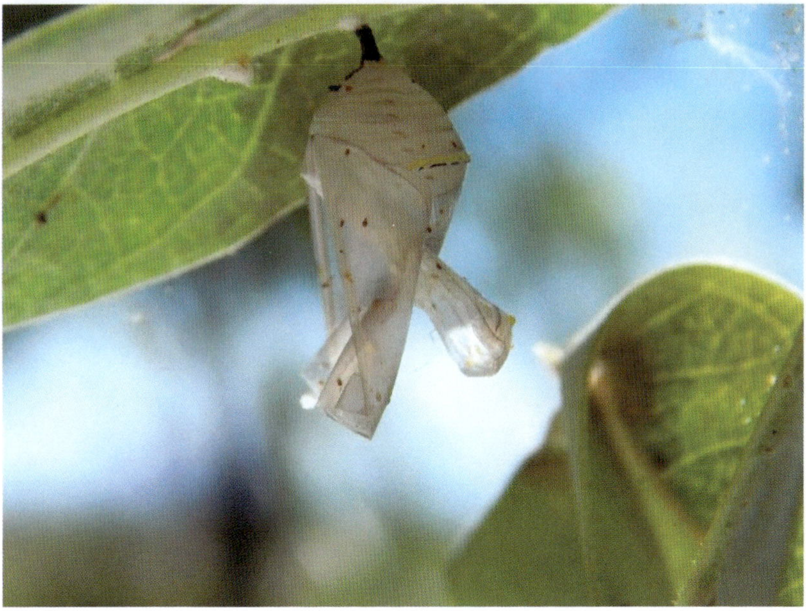

34

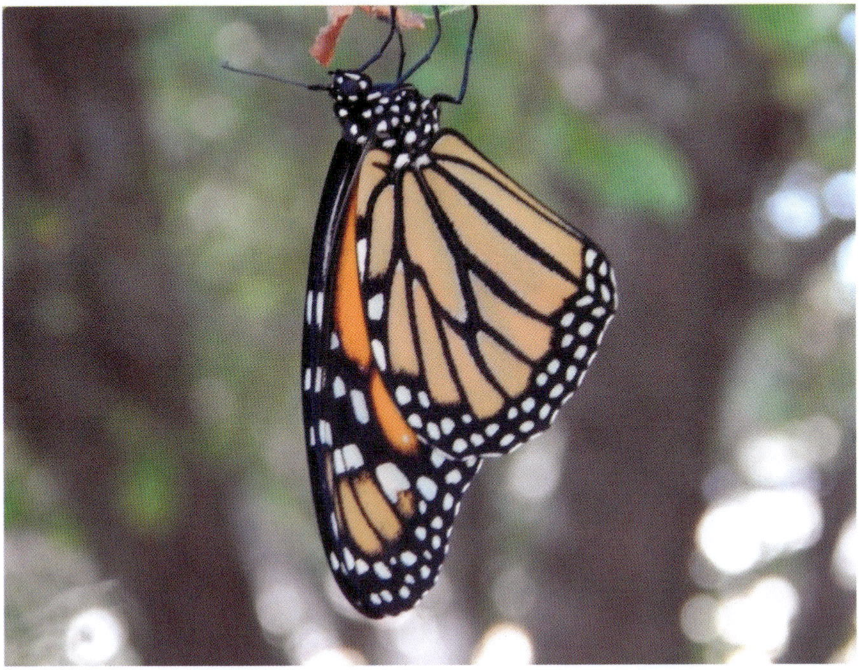

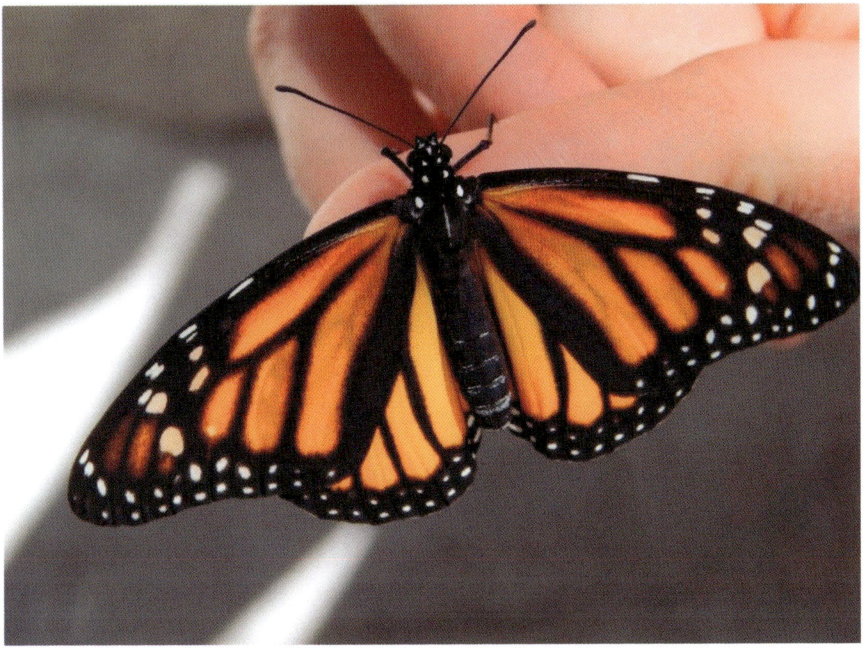

I believe this is not only a representation of a chrysalis, but is also symbolic of an acorn.

Oak Leaves

The Order of the American Knights likely chose their name based on the symbolism of the Oak. This group was also known as the Sons of Liberty who were primarily active during the American Civil War. The abbreviation would be S.O.L. which ties the Latin word for sun. King **Sol**omon is also tied to many of the sites I've studied.

Transmutation
Notice the final stage appears to be phallic.

Ouroboros
Illustration From
The Chrysopoeia of Cleopatra

In Greek, **"ἕν τὸ πᾶν"** means *"hen to pān"* or *"One is everything"*
"The All Is One"

The term **chrysopoeia** (in alchemy) means transmutation into gold. (Ancient Greek: χρυσοποιία, *khrusopoiia* from the Greek χρυσός, *khrusos*, "gold", and ποιεῖν, *poiein*, "to make"). It is symbolic of the creation of the Stone of the Philospher's and the completion of the Great Work.

38

Ouroboros
Drawing by Theodoros Pelecanos, 1478

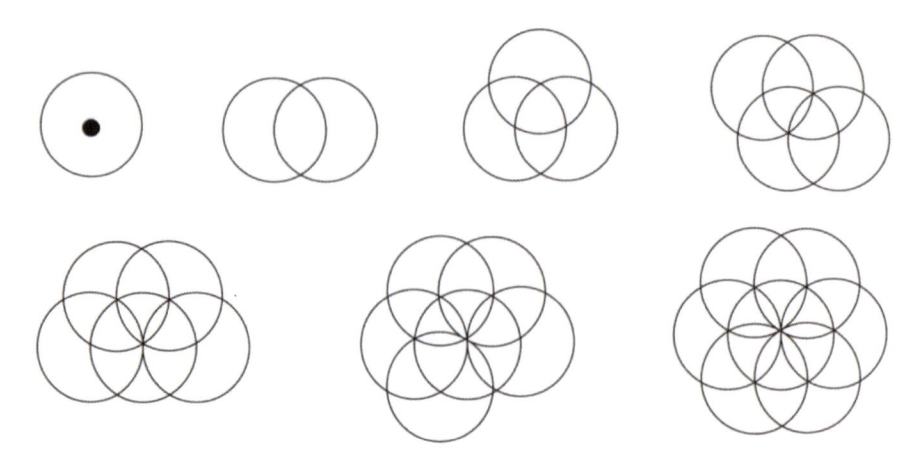

The Seven Days of Creation can be found portrayed in the seed of life. This is similar to a fertilized egg.

I've heard it said that upon conception there is a spark of light.

Some of the meanings of the circumpunct are:

God ---To the Greek philosophers and the Pythagoreans.
Sun --- To the astrologers and astronomers.
Gold --- To the alchemist.
The Spirit --- To the Ojibwa

Some other possible meanings are:
The Son of God
Christ
The Seed
The Bull's Eye Target
The Phallus
Shaft
Air
Something Contained Here
Ra
The number one
The number three
Central Point
Entered Apprentice Freemason
I AM
The Compass
Axis Mundi
Polar Axis

Masonic Tracing Board

According to some sources of information. One of the meanings of the symbolism of the point within a circle are: the point is the individual brother and the circle is the boundary of his duty to God and man, and he shouldn't allow his own personal interests or passions betray him.

Manley Hall stated:
"The dot, being most proximate to perfection, is the simplest, and therefore the least imperfect of all symbols."

I was thinking about the opposing directions of the circumpunct- one that goes inward like a black hole, and the other goes outward towards growth and expansion and seems to be linked to the Primordial Mound where all existence began. This principle seems to be everywhere around us, we must create or disintigrate. Expansion and growth, or death and decay. This is seems to be true with our mentality as well. We can have an abundance mentality, or have a lack mentality. One thought process will give us the energy and the faith to go forward towards progress while the other thought process will make us discouraged and degress.

In Mackey's book, *The symbolism of Freemasonry*, it states:
"Now, this hermaphrodism of the Supreme Divinity was again supposed to be represented by the sun, which was the male generative energy, and by nature, or the universe, which was the female prolific principle. **And this union was symbolized in different ways, but principally by the point within a circle, the point indicating the sun, and the circle the universe, invigorated and fertilized by his generative rays. And in some of the Indian cave-temples, this**

allusion was made more manifest by the inscription of the signs of the zodiac on the circle."

But the two perpendicular parallel lines remain to be explained. Everyone is familiar with the very recent interpretation, that they represent the two Saints John, the Baptist and the Evangelist. But this modern exposition must be abandoned, if we desire to obtain the true ancient signification.

In the first place, we must call to mind the fact that, at two particular points of his course, the sun is found in the zodiacal signs of Cancer (June) and Capricorn (December).

These points are astronomically distinguished as the summer and winter solstice. When the sun is in these points, he has reached his greatest northern and southern declination, (a gradual falling off from a higher state) and produces the most evident effects on the temperature of the seasons, and on the length of the days and nights.

These points, if we suppose the circle to represent the sun's apparent course, will be indicated by the points where the parallel lines touch the circle, or, in other words, the parallels will indicate the limits of the sun's extreme northern and southern declination, when he arrives at the solstitial points of Cancer and Capricorn.

But the days when the sun reaches these points are, respectively, the 21st of June and the 22nd of December, and this will account for their subsequent application to the two Saints John, whose anniversaries have been placed by the church near those days."

Point Within A Circle in Egypt: The 2 vertical lines on the sides of the Point Within a Circle symbol date back before Solomon. On early Egyptian monuments there have been found the Alpha and Omega, (the symbol of God as the beginning and the end.), in the center of the circle bordered by 2 upright, perpendicular parallel serpents.

Geometry hides in plain sight many complex mathematical relationships. The circle is perhaps the most natural representation of Unity. Sometimes it is presented with a dot in the middle (the symbol of the Monad) which refers to the Tao, the essence of all Creation.

My personal journey message from the circumpunct, is to start where I am with what I have and go from there. I have the seeds of greatness in me. Continue to expand and to refine myself and to share my light with the world. (Which light is given to me from Christ and my connection to Him.) There is an infinite abundance as long as I share and expand outwards. However, the opposite is true as to the infinite void that will never be filled if it is taken in reverse.

The Compass
From Seaman's Secrets by John Davis, 1594

Notice the spiral to the side of the circumpunct. The spiral has similar ties to the circumpunct. Often the spiral can be used as a directional. Also, the extra circles around the circumpunct can add extra meaning, sometimes distance, depth, or amounts depending on many factors.

In Chris Hegg's book *"Ancient Universal Language of Man"* he mentions his thoughts on seasons and shows a good example of how some of these symbols with the extra circles, such as the circle within the circle with the dot, (like the one above) perhaps means "winter" at some sites.

Chris also mentions that, in sign language the hand gestures are similar to this drawing as for the meaning of "expansion."

47

48

There is a lot of information portayed here. Notice the symbols incorporated into this image.

Notice the usage of the ram (or goat). Notice it's horns are in the shape of a doorway or an ark shape. Notice the centaur-looking king wearing a crown and the ram's horns are his chest. Notice the mouth of the snake which is also the king's right hand. Notice the king's face and crown are a foot.

49

50

This circle of railroad spikes and a bolt in the center was found at the beginning of a suspect cache site. Without thinking, we took the spikes home. But when we got home and counted them, we realized there were 13 and suspected they were a marker used by modern cache guardians.(I suspect belonging to The Knights of the Golden Circle.) So we hurried and returned them to the exact same location. However, when we went back again, they were gone.

Some of the modern "graffiti" can be tied to information at cache, mineral or sacred sites. Many of the sites are still being updated, and guarded. It appears the reason for the newer "graffiti" is often tied to the reason the older writings are at these locations. It takes some investigation to determine if modern markings are tied to mine or vault sites. Usually, it is fairly easy for someone who knows how to read and follow symbols and markers to know what to disregard. A good detective will look at, and catalog ALL clues regardless of age. Pay attention to EVERYTHING. The newer information may be easier for some people to grasp and comprehend.

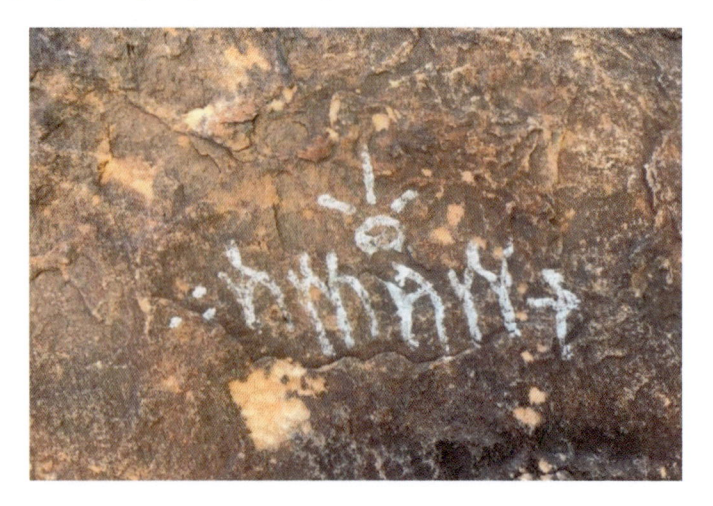

Notice the circumpunct. Also notice the word Chiropractor. This modern writing shed light on many of the older writings here and what they are about. There are drawings of the spine. (The human spine has 33 vertabrae and in the Occult is sometimes called the serpent.)

A portion of a spine

53

The Spine

The djed from ancient Egypt is a pillar-like symbol found in Egyptian hieroglyphics and is asociated with Osiris the Egyptian god of the underworld and the afterlife and the resurrection. It is said the djed represents the spine of Osiris.

The Djed

55

Notice what appears to be many stylized versions of the spine (axis mundi) principle. Also notice the "turkey tracks" seem to be incorporated into the spine meaning. I suspect what many people call turkey tracks, are actually benu-bird tracks. The *Ardea bennuides* is an extinct type of heron which is thought to be the bennu or benu-bird. It is said to have created itself from fire. The cry of the benu-bird is said to have marked the begining of time. Thoth is associated with the benu-bird as Thoth was said to have measured and recorded time. The benu-bird is known as, "He who came into being by himself." The benu-bird is said to represent the first life to appear on the primordial mound (the benben) out of the waters of chaos.

The benben and the benu-bird are from the same root word, "Bn" which means, "ascension" and, "to rise." The word "weben" is thought to have come from the same roots as well and means, "to shine." In the Egyptian book of the dead, the benu is called the ba-soul of Ra. It is also said to be a symbol of Osiris. It is said to represent Atum as the Life and light of the world. The benu-bird is thought to be the prototype for the phoenix. The habitat of the modern-day heron (like the benu) is along the shores of watery areas, and its tracks are easy to be seen in the mud. I belive the "turkey tracks" or the benu-bird tracks drawn on the rocks are often associated with directionals.

This appears to me, to be a symbolic drawing of a vertabrae and portion of the spinal cord.
(Photo courtesy: Daniel Lowe)

In human anatomy, the craniovertebral junction is where your head and neck meet. This area is made of the occipital bone, the atlas and the axis. The atlas is the very utmost part of the spine with the axis just below it. This area is responsible for most of the spine's rotation.

The spine is a central symbol

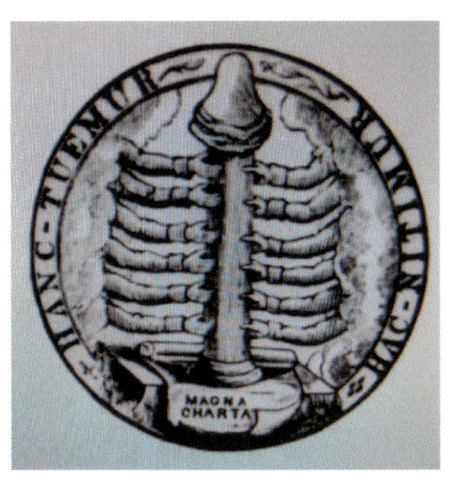

Magna Carta Libertatum

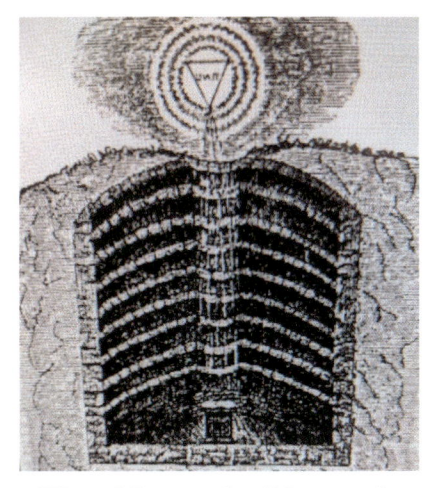

**The Masonic Manual
by Robert Macoy**

Occiput
Atlas
Axis
Cervical Vertebrae

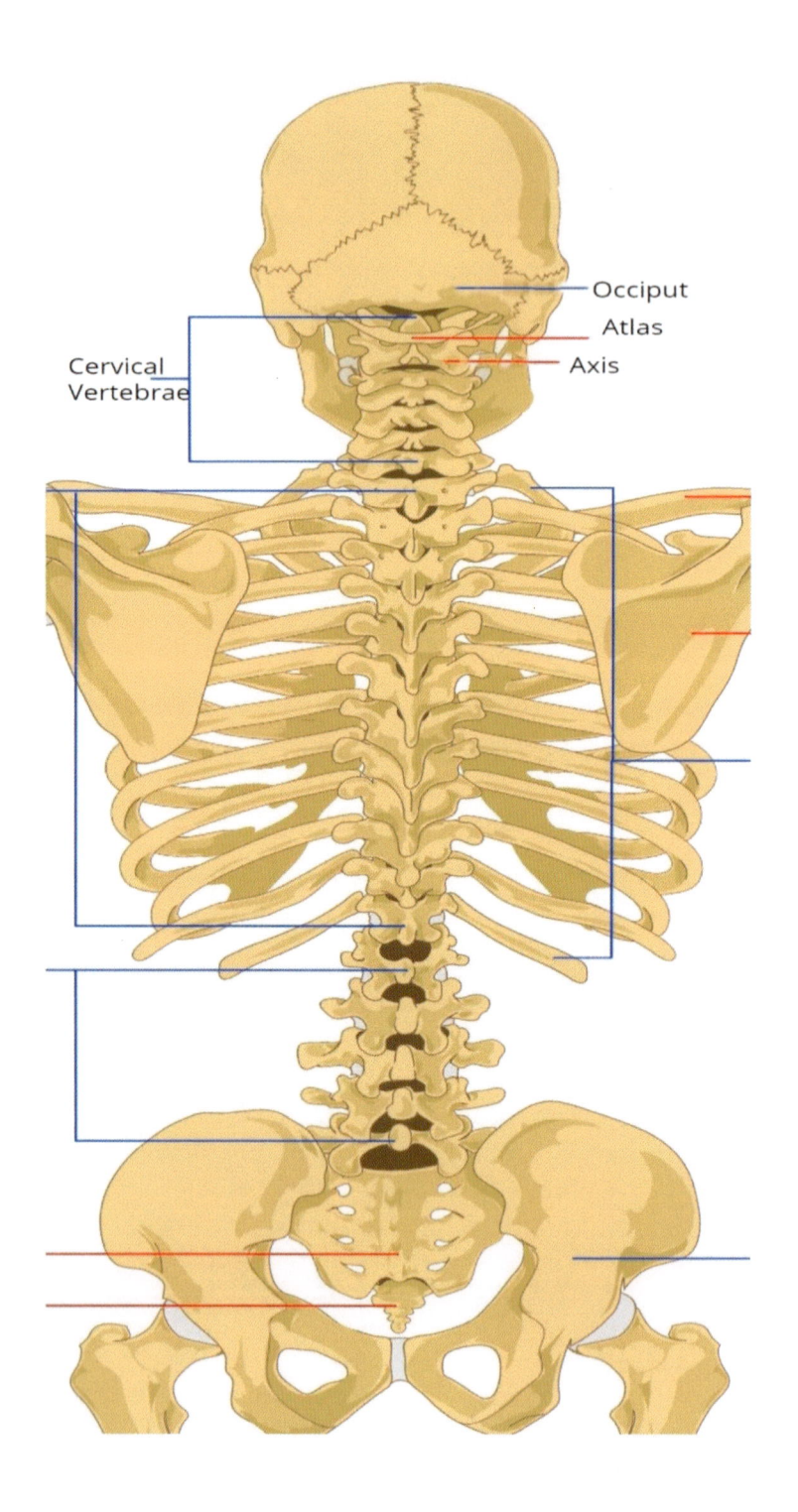

*The Latin prefix **Chiro** is from ancient Greek χείρ (kheir) which means **hand**.*

In Greek mythology, the centar **Chiron** (/ˈkaɪrən/ KY-rən) Χείρων ("hand") was known by his brethren as being the wisest and most just.

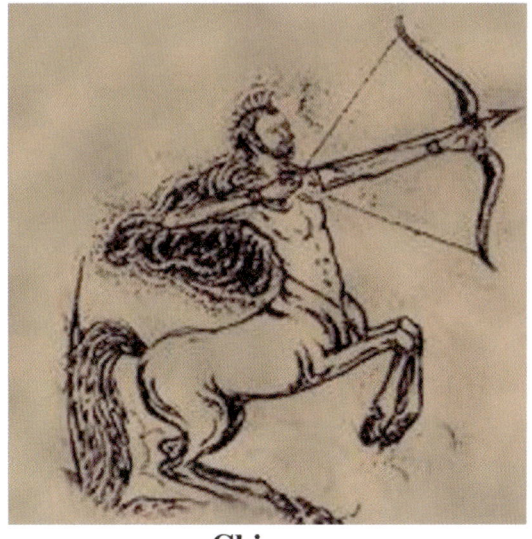

Chiron
(By McAnndra)

The Chi-Rho

The Chi-Rho is known as a symbol of Christ. It is known as one of the earliest forms of the Chrismon. This is also known as the Christogram, as it is a monogram of Chi (X) and Rho (P).

ΧΡΙΣΤΟΣ (Greek)= XP

In treasure hunting, we have all heard X marks the spot. Usually this isn't the case, at least not in the way that most people would think. But X will often mark the spot for those who know how to see, and who understand how to read the symbols. X will often be a clue.

Also notice how the X is made of the two opposing symbols. It is also the hourglass. The XP for Christogram is also the starting symbols for Gold and Christ in Greek.

The Axis Mundi is often portrayed as a tree
(Painting by Stefan Duncan)

The Tree of Life is an important symbol in nearly all cultures. Its roots go downwards into the earth and its branches reach up to the heavens while it dwells on the earth. It portrays its existence in heaven, earth and the underworld. It is a uniting of the above and the below.

The Axis Mundi is a symbol representing the center of the world where heaven connects with the earth. Different groups of people represent the Axis Mundi with varied symbols. Some of these symbols may include things found in nature such as a mountain, a tree, a rainbow, or a column of smoke.

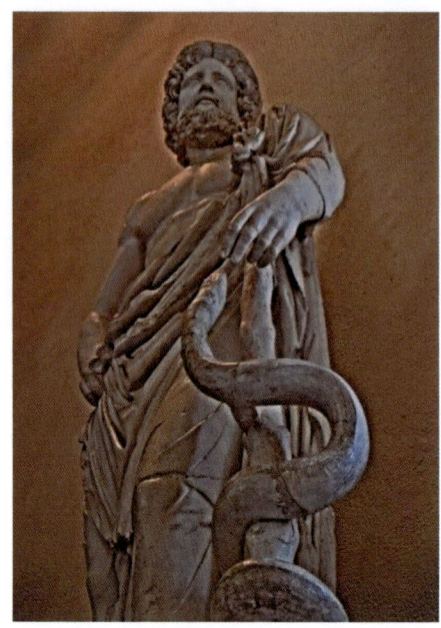

The Rod of Asclepius. Asclepius was the Greek God of Medicine

The serpent on the rod is often the symbol of medicine and health.
I find it interesting that the symbol of the serpent is used to symbolize both Christ and Satan.
In Mesoamerica, Quetzalcoatl, the feathered serpent, was used as a symbol of a great white God who visited their ancestors.

I also find it interesting that in the sciptures, when the symbol of the serpent is used as Christ, it is mentioned as being "lifted up."
Christ referred to the lifting up of the serpent as a symbol of Himself being lifted on the cross.
Quetzalcoatl was mentioned as the feathered (or plumed) serpent, and I believe this implies the same meaning as being lifted up. Feathers are generally a symbol of being lifted to a higher plane.
Christ overcame the serpent. He overcame death and hell and the grave. He overcame the serpent.

Hermes

The Symbol of Mercury

CAIRNS

    Hermes (Hermarines) the Greek God, was known as *Mercury* to the Romans. *Mercury* is derived from Latin "merx", which means "merchandise" and is tied to the origins of the words ""commerce, and merchant." Hermes is mentioned in old manuscript legends as being one of the founders of Freeemasonry. He was said to have found one of two pillars with the science enscribed on it and taught it to others. He is said to be the father of wisdom. He is also known as a soul guide and a messenger of the Gods. He is also known as a trickster.
In some accounts Pan is said to have been the son of Hermes.

66

Most scholars believe that *Hermes* is derived from Greek ἕρμα "herma" meaning *cairn* or *stone heap*.
According to wikkipedia, the stone etymology is also linked to Indo-European *ser- to bind, put together.*

A symbol of the Axis Mundi

The term *axis mundi* comes from the Latin words "*axis*" (pivot point, or line) and "mundi"(world).
The Axis Mundi is often described as the center point, the point where heaven meets earth, where communication between heaven and earth can exist.

A few objects also known to represent the Axis Mundi can be a staff, staircase, cross, steeple, pillar, spire, wheel's hub, and ladder. Many places that are considered holy are where people feel the closest to heaven and feel that link between heaven and earth. Often these places are places of worship, and will give people a more eternal perspective on life.

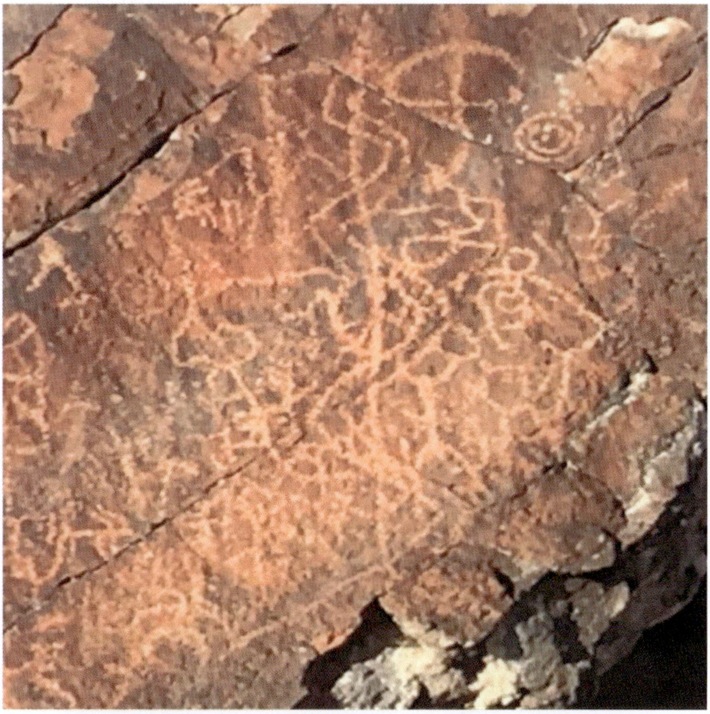

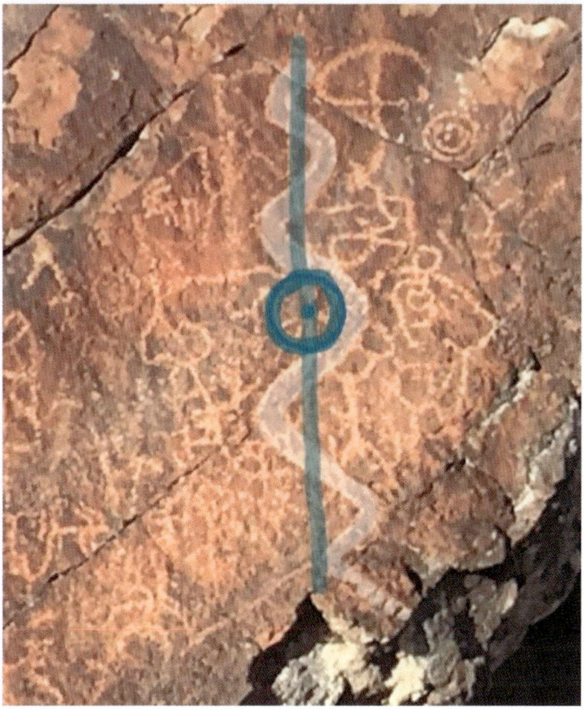

Portland, Oregon Temple

I Nephi 8 mentions an account of the Tree of Life, and I Nephi 11 contains an interpretaion of that vision.

Big Horn Medicine Wheel in Wyoming
(Photo credit, Imerriot)

The 1581 Bünting Clover Leaf Map

    This old map depicts Jerusalem as the center of the world. Many cultures consider their homeland as the Axis Mundi.

As can be seen in this map, a location can also be considered as an Axis Mundi.

Isodore's Etymologiae T and O Map

Some people believed that after Noah's flood, Ham, Shem and Japheth colonized these three outer locations and Jerusalem was the center.

中国

China is known as 中国, or the 'Middle Kingdom'. At around 1000 BC, the Chou people believed their empire occupied the middle of the earth and was surrounded by barbarians. Throughout the ages, many cultures have believed that they are the center of civilization. The ancient Egyptians thought of their land as the center of the world which was ruled by Order. Chaos reigned in the lands beyond their borders.

The Flammarion Engraving

Some trees that have been symbolic of the Axis Mundi are:

The Tree of Knowledge of Good and Evil. (Mentioned in the Bible.)
The Tree of Life (Depicted thoughtout various cultures.)
Yggdrasil (In old Norse it is a gigantic Ash tree also known as the "World Tree".)
The Date Palm
The Evergreen
The Oak

The Date Palm and the (Bennu) Phoenix
(From Juan de Horozco's Sacra Symbola 1601)

Bennu is related to the Ancient Egyptian word "wbn" (weben) meaning "rise" or "shine."

Sometimes the Bennu is shown perched on the top stone of the pyramid called the benben stone. The benben stone is the capstone of the pyramid and is said to symbolize the primordial mound that came out of the waters where the first rays of light were shown.

75

Kabbalah Tree of Life

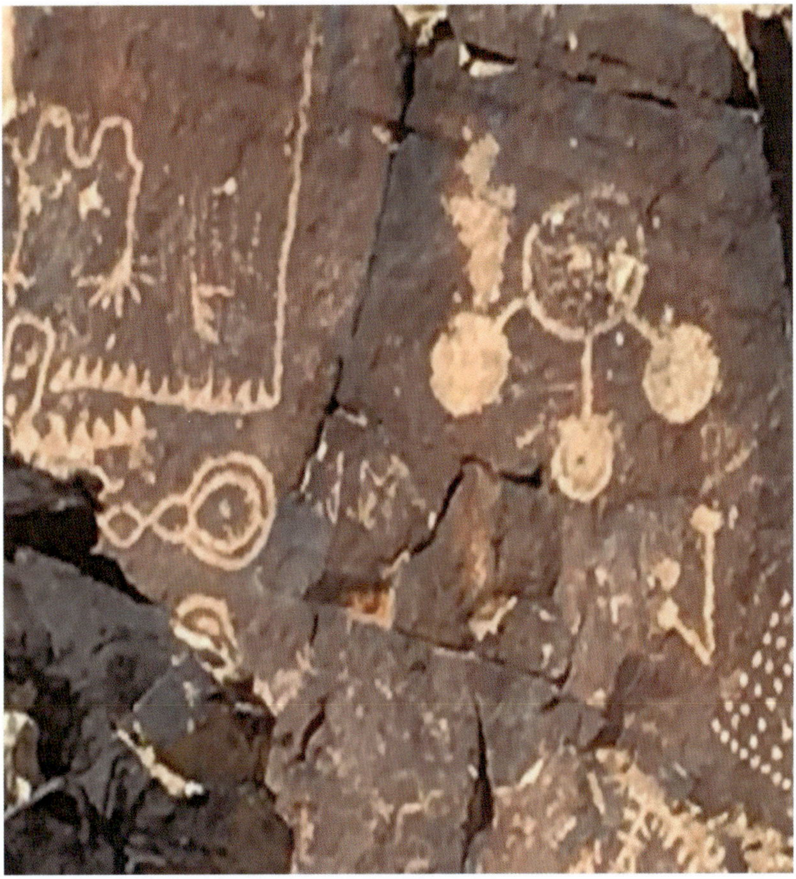

I believe this is a representation of the Axis Mundi

Revisiting the chiro and one of the meanings of the hand, I would like to show some examples of the hidden hand that can be found at many important sites near information points.

Can you see the hidden hand?

The Malam writing, mentioned later in this book, is not visible in this photo, but it is near the thumb. I think the hand is actually palm side up.

From another viewpoint, the thumb is a phallic symbol. And from the backside, the thumb is a turtle's head. (It smiles, and has an eye during winter solsitce.)

This is a slightly different viewpoint of the previous picture.

There is a lot of information from this viewpoint. Some of you won't be able to see anything here, but for those who can see, here are a few things to look for:
*The X
*The 7
*The Compass and Square
*The small hand, palm side up (right below the king's arm)
*The King sitting on his throne
*The woman's face next to the king. (Looks to be Athena or a queen.)

More examples of hands.

Yod

Yod represents the dot where all creation begins.
Yod is considered the spirit or the spark in all things.
Yod is the 10th letter in Hebrew= The number of Completion.

Yod (Paleo)

Yod also means "Hand."
Yod is considered the starting point of the
presence of God in all things.

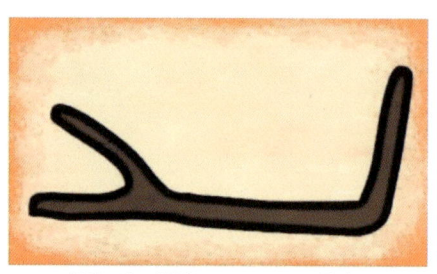

Yod (Pictograph)

Yod is Symbolic of Power and Possesion.
It is the smallest of all of the letters in the Hebrew alphabet.
In Jewish tradition Yod represents just a dot and a divine
point of energy.

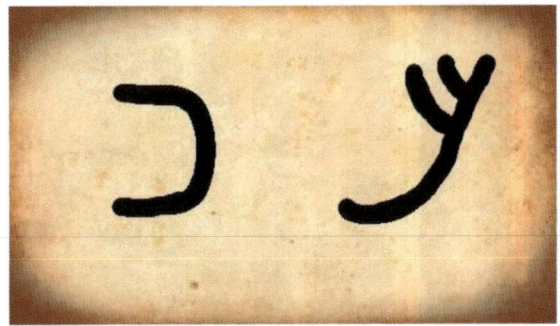

Kaph (Pictograph)
Kaph (Modern)   **Kaph (Paleo)**

    The meaning of the yod and Kaph are very similar. The Kaph is the palm of the hand or the bent hand, while the yod is the arm or hand, which is similar to Egyptian heiroglyphics.

    According to my research, William Tyndale translated the meaning of atonement into the 1526 English Bible from the Hebrew word "Kaphar." *Wikipedia*'s entry on the word "atonement" mentioned that William Tyndale thought that if the meaning behind "*kaphar*" were translated as "reconciliation," there would be a pervasive misunderstanding of the word's deeper significance to not just reconcile, but "to cover," so the word "atonement" was invented.

    Christ has us covered. He made the reconciliation between God the Father and Man. He made it so that we can be purified so that we can dwell again in the presence of God.

Another word that relates to what I have seen at cache and vault sites is one that made me shudder when I first read it out on the rocks, but it has a meaning that should be mentioned here. The word "Occult" means, "covered over," and also has the meaning of "to hide," and " to conceal."

To me it appears that many of the occult groups not only conceal and hide meanings within their teachings and symbols, but they veil this information so that their higher members can have the understanding of how to reopen their vault or cache sites.

I find it interesting that the word "Kaphar" which is often translated as "Atonement" has a similar meaning to Occult when tied to vault sites. These words have always been polar opposites in my mind.

I learned early on, that the people who set up many of these sites used many languages, and loved etymology. They loved looking at things through as many perspectives as possible. Sometimes a message will be written upside down or backwards. Sometimes it will be reversed. Sometimes it will be an anagram. Often they will use symbols. Many of the symbols are something that can be understood by someone thousands of years later.

They will also try to be deceptive in what they write to lead someone who does not understand in the wrong direction. From what I have read in books, and seen first hand symbolized at many of these sites, I believe that many of these places have been trapped and were not made to get into unless you know for sure what you are doing.

Latin	Hebrew		Aramaic		Greek	
A alef	⚔	א	1	ox	alpha	A
B beth	ℬ	ב	2	house	beta	B
G gimel	⏋	ג	3	camel	gamma	Γ
D daleth	△	ד	4	door	delta	Δ
H hay	ョ	ה	5	window	hoi	H
U uau	Y	ו	6	hook	**upsilon**	Y
Z zayin	⊃	ז	7	weapon	zeta	Z
CH heth	H	ח	8	fence	(h)eta	H
T teth	⊗	ט	9	winding	theta	Θ
Y yod	ㄥ	׳	10	hand	iota	I
K kaph	ש	כ	20	bent hand	kappa	K
L lamed	∠	ל	30	goad	lambda	Λ
M mem	ツ	מ	40	water	mu	M
N nun	ソ	נ	50	fish	nu	N
S samek	⨦	ס	60	prop	xei	Ξ
E/A ayin	O	ע	70	eye	omega	Ω
P pe	⊃	פ	80	mouth	pei	Π
TS tsadee	⊢	צ	90	hook	zeta	Z
Q koph	⋔	ק	100	needle eye	chi	X
R resh	⊲	ר	200	head	rho	P
SH shin	W	ש	300	tooth	sigma	Σ
T tau	X	ת	400	mark	tau	T

This hidden hand is part of an information point that shows other pieces of information when viewed from different perspectives.

88

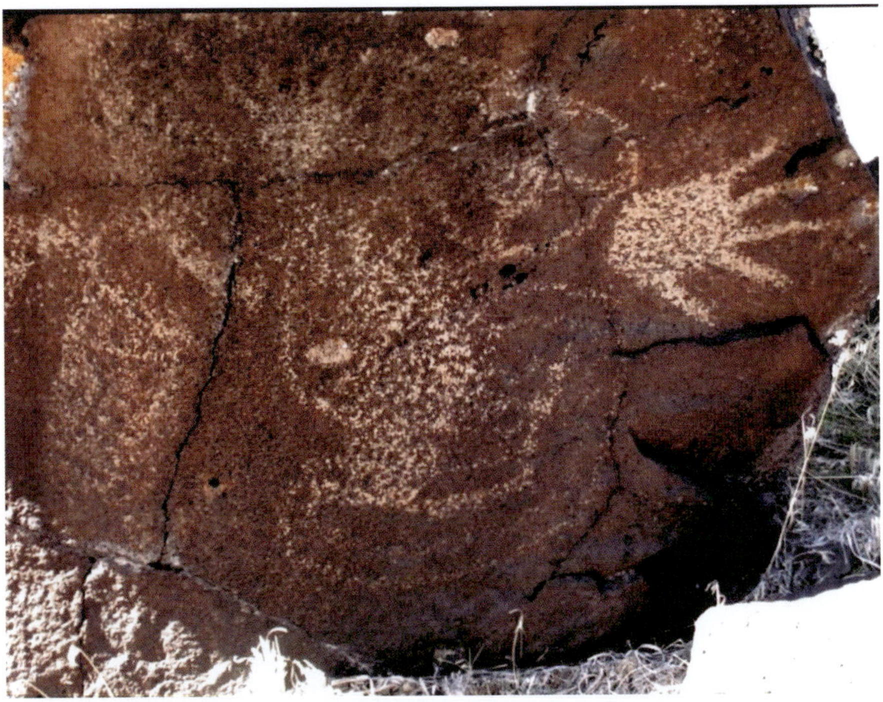

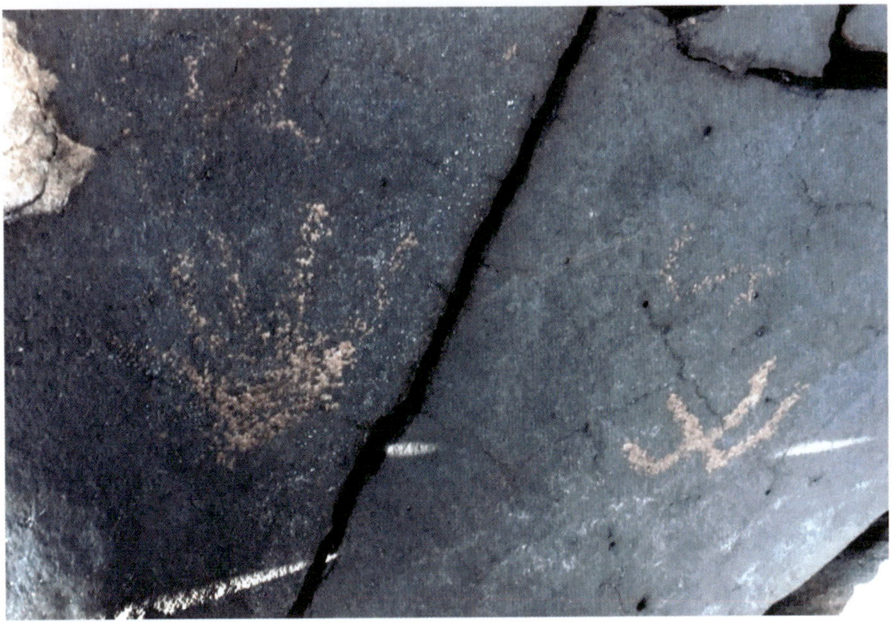

Chalk Creek Mysteryglyph Panel
Fillmore, Utah

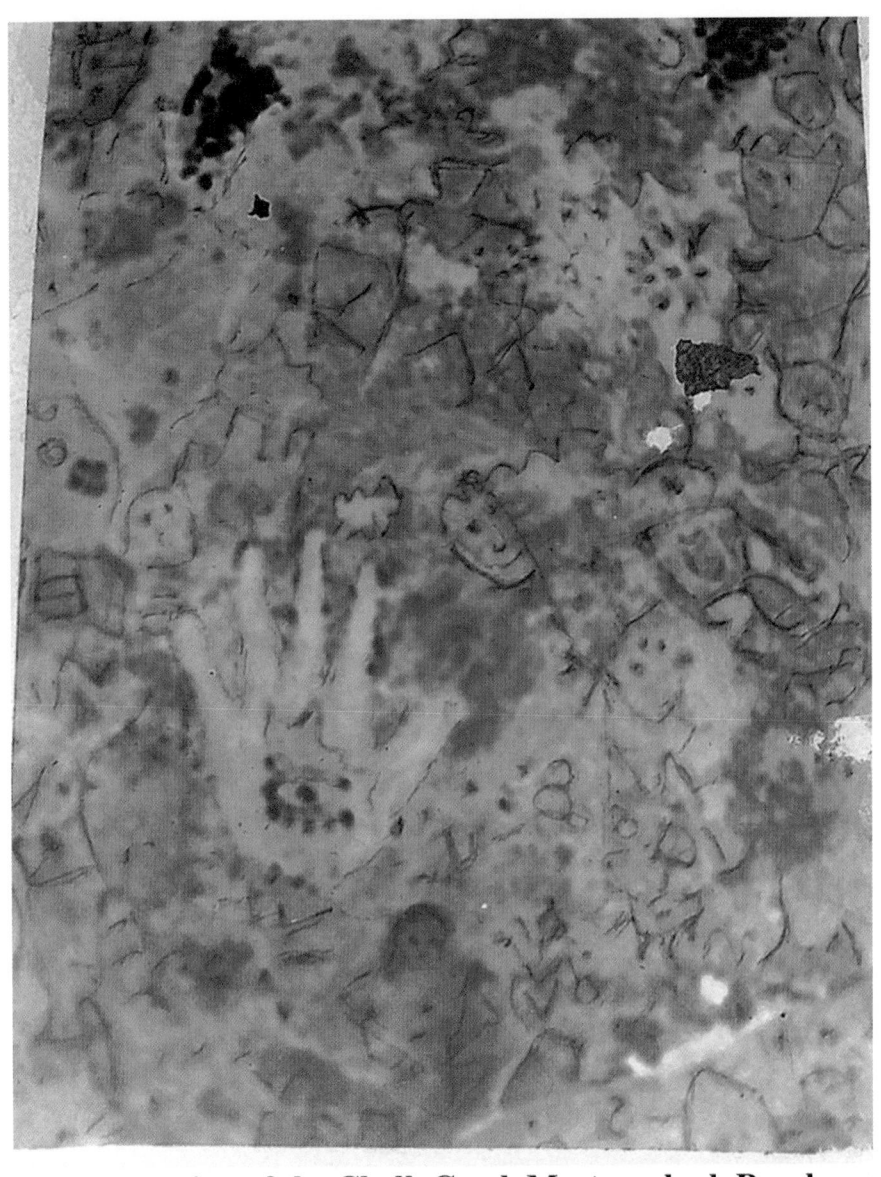

**A portion of the Chalk Creek Mysteryglyph Panel
as it appeared when Frank Beckwith took this photo.**
(Photo credit, Beckwith Family)

This portion of the panel was taken from its original location, and is currently behind the Forest Service building in Fillmore.
Not much of it is left to see.

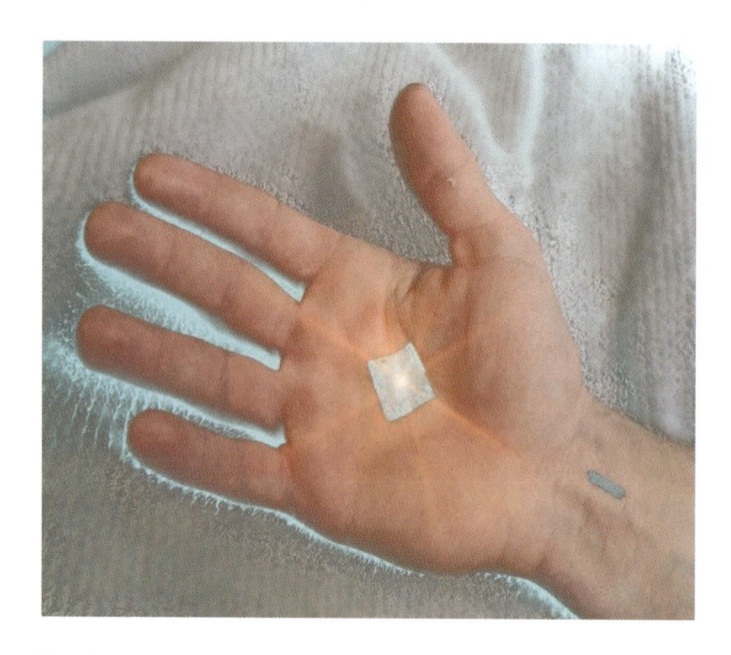

The "punct" found at vault sites, I believe is symbolic of the wounds in Christ's hands. It is the shape that is in the center of the compass and square as well. In the Bible in John 10:9-10 it says, "I am the door: by me if any man enter in, he shall be saved, and shall go in and out, and find pasture. The thief cometh not, but for to steal, and to kill, and to destroy: I am come that they might have life, and that they might have it more abundantly."

I have seen the yod shape also used at vault sites, but it doesn't seem to be as common as it is likely harder to create.

The Nail can be symbolic of the Axis Mundi

The 6th letter of the Hebrew alphabet is the Vav. It is symbolic of the nail.
It stands for uniting or joining two objects together. The vav symbolizes a connector and is a bridge between the above and the below. It symbolizes union of the soul and the body. When used in a sentence, the vav is a connector and is used as the word, "and."
The Vav is the male princple and is considered phallic.
Vav represents the number of man since man was created on the 6th day. It is the capstone of creation.
The 6 is said to be associated with a death trap when found at certain cache sites created by the Jesuits or others of the similar beliefs.

Vav- Uau- Waw (Modern Hebrew)
Looks like the nail

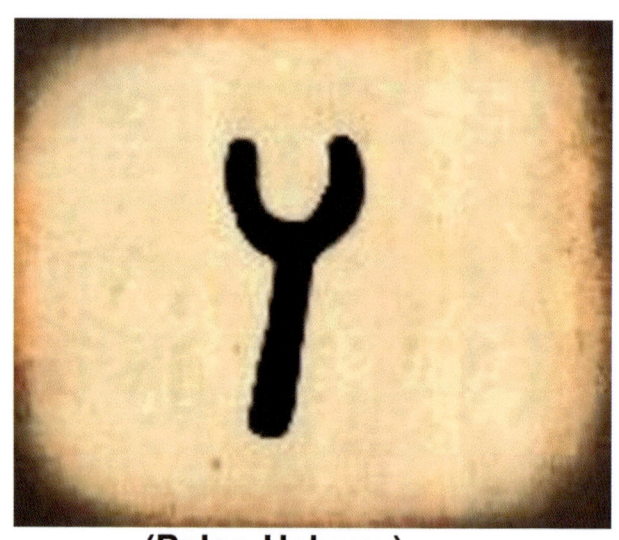

(Paleo Hebrew)
Looks like a tent peg

Sometimes, important information is done with shadow or with light.

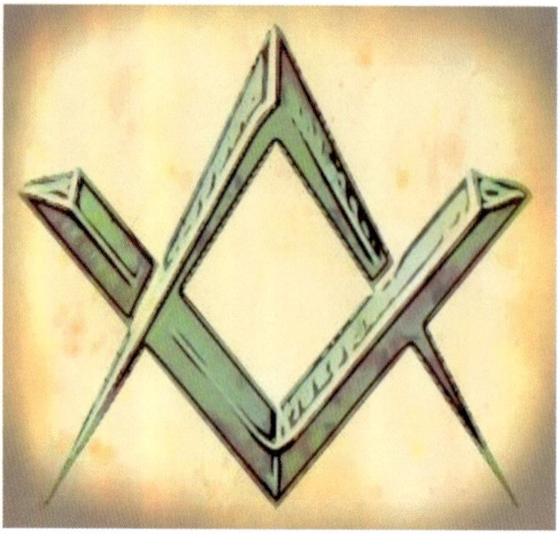

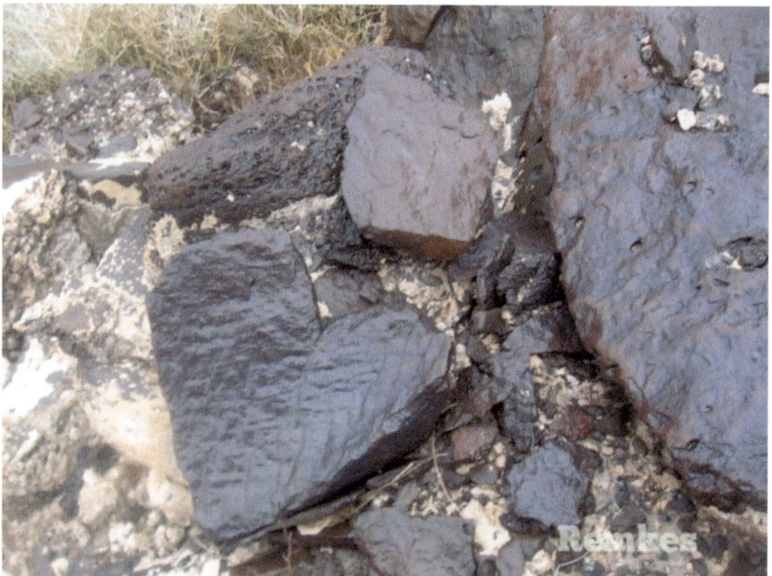

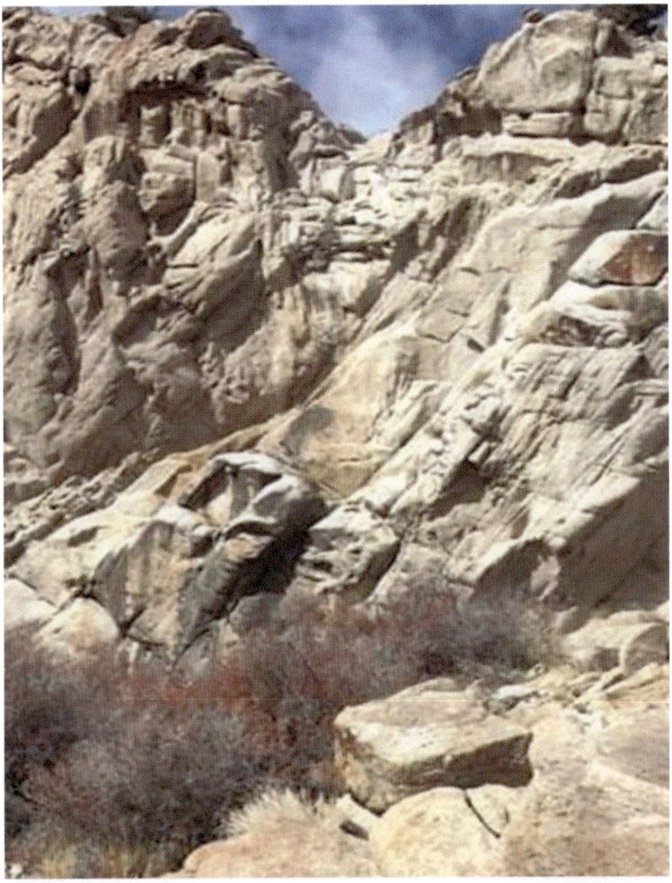

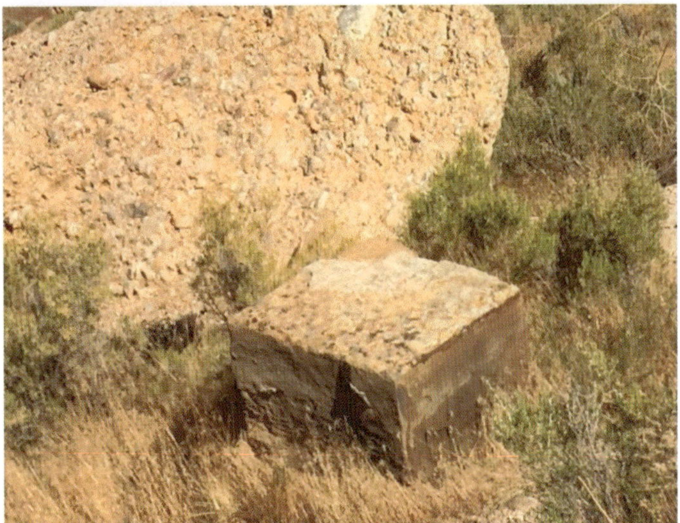

98

99

Becoming The Perfect Ashlar

The Shriner's Emblem

    I originally was confused by this, as I thought there looked to be a fossilized spine of some large animal encased in this volcanic rock. Then I thought it looked like some old brickwork that maybe a volcano had erupted over and the lava hadn't melted. But then, I remembered I was following the symbols and rock markers and the chance of either of those things being in the lava were not likely. Notice the little slice mark just below the perfect square that goes into the rock. To me, it looks like they used something like a heat torch to create this. Also notice the counter-relief area just below the symbolic spine. Notice that this looks like the blade of a scimiter. (With emphasis on the tip.)

The scimiter happens to be symbolic of the backbone of some fraternities and their members. Some societies, such as the Shriner's (which were also known as the Ancient Arabic Order of the Nobles of the Mystic Shrine) used the scimiter to symbolize the spine.

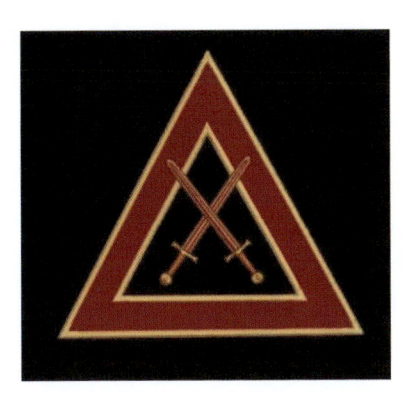

Sentinel Badge of the Royal Arch Masons
The point is the sharp end of a sword, knife or arrow.

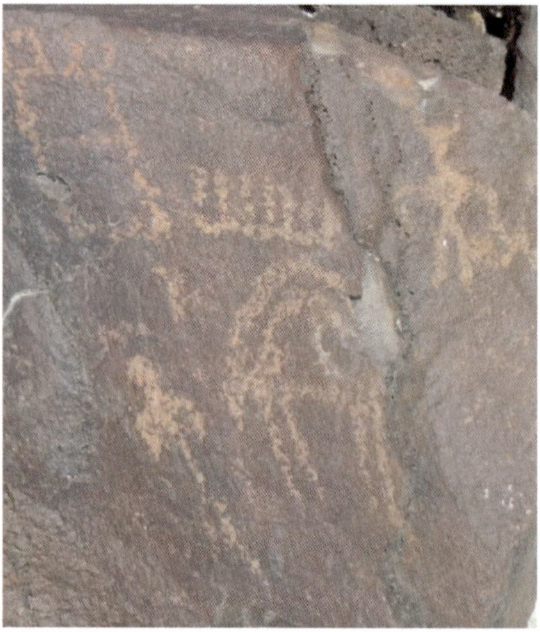

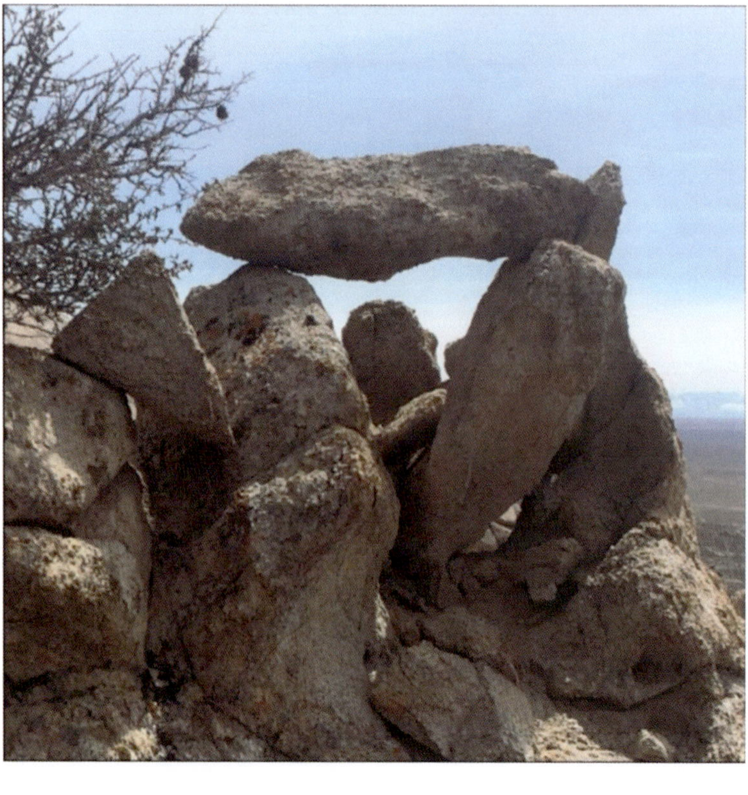

The 7th letter of the Hebrew alphabet is zayin. Its meaning goes back to a sharp sword or sharp weapon. The 7th letter is also symbolic of the day God rested. When it is seen at a site, it is said the Spanish used this to signify a resting spot, but it appears some of the older cultures used this to symbolize a resting spot as in what we would say, "Rest In Peace". It is also important to remember that 7 is number symbolic of Gold.

Ashlar

Look back at the photo of *Becoming the Perfect Ashlar*. Notice how the center square in is perfect, and looks like a brick ready to be used for building with, while the others are in various degrees of becoming. I believe this is symbolic of becoming the perfect Ashlar.

According to some definitions, an Ashlar is a square stone for building or paving and comes from Old French *aisseler*. It is from Medieval Latin *arsella* meaning *a beam or shingle*, diminutive of Latin *assis* is also spelled as *axis*.

Opposing Vs
Notice the V notch and the pyramid shape.

As with most symbols there are many layers of meanings.
One is pointing upwards and the other downwards.
-As above, so below-
-Male and Female-
-Opposites-
-V-

In the next few images, I have included some examples of different V and pyramid markers. Some are very old, and are very large. Others are smaller as I am closer to the target.

107

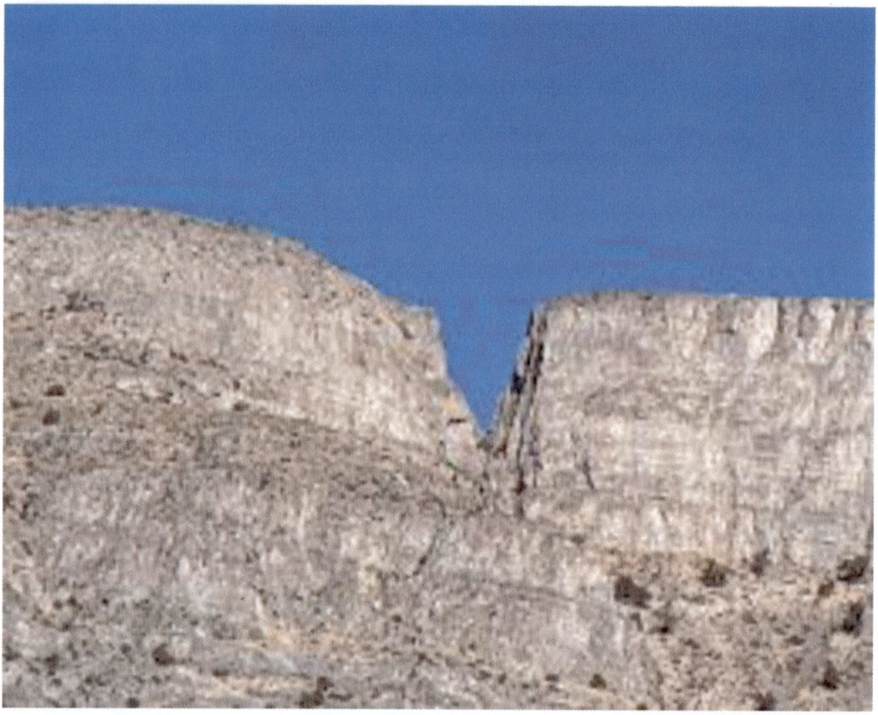

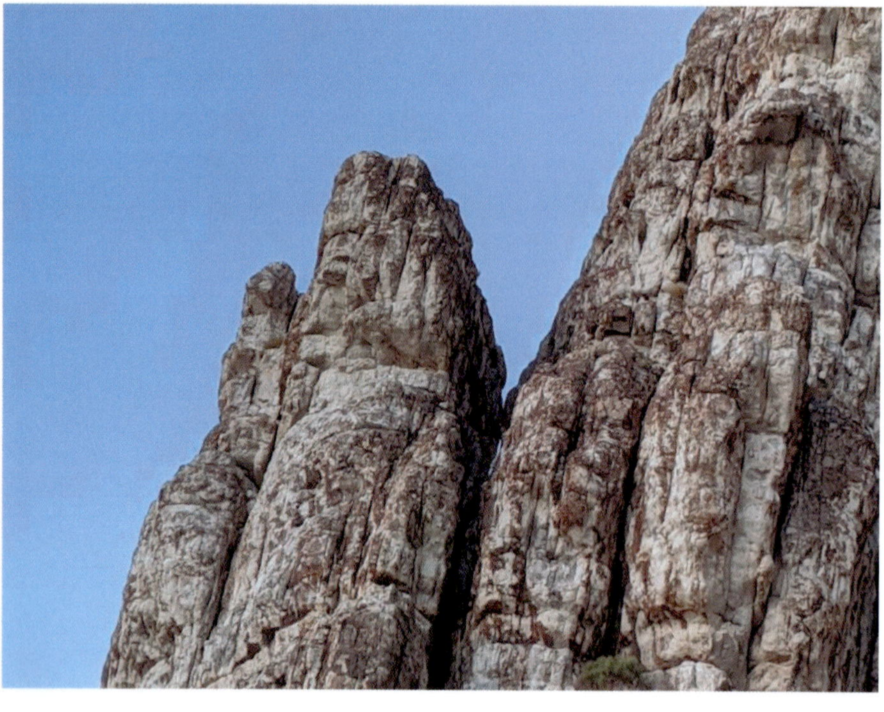

Parowan Gap

As Above

So Below

When these opposing triangles come together, this forms the compass and square as seen in freemasonry. Simply put, the compass is a tool used to create a circle, and the square is a tool used for marking a 90 degree angle. (A mitre square is used for 45 degree angles.)

One of the possible meanings of the as above so below could mean:
The sun is above= And the sun is below= Sun symbol=Gold

"Twain in One" and other similar phrases seem to be tied to this concept. But from the beginning of the creation God made them male and female. And they twain shall be one flesh: so then they are no more twain, but one flesh. -Mark 10: 6&8 The New Testament.

I find it intersting that in prospecting, the best mineral areas tend to be where the two opposing colors or types of rock come together. The concept of creation seems to be tied in opposites, and seems to be the center of the two opposing forces. Perhaps that is why we needed to have this mortal experience with all of the opposing forces and difficult trials. We have the opportunity to become.

E Pluribus Unum
Latin for "out of many, one."

E Pluribus Unum was put on American Currency and used as the National Motto until the mid 1950s when it was replaced with "In God We Trust." It was first used on the $5.00 Heraldic Eagle gold coin in 1795, and was used on some Continental coins, which were already falling away from a gold backed currency. In 1787, the Fugio penny had a sun and sundial on the front and on the back it had the saying, "We are One."

An example of a (replica) of a Continental Coin
"We are One"

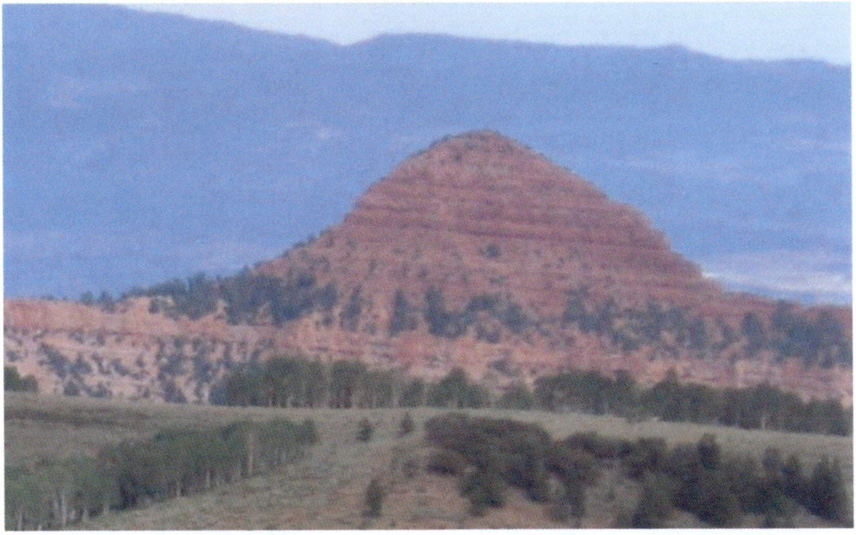

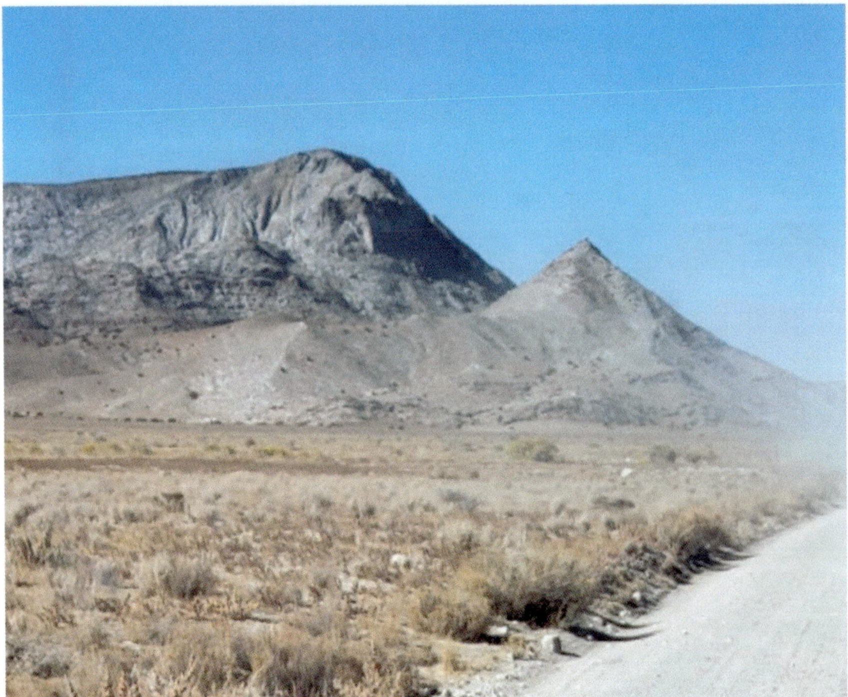

If you look to the alphabet, you will see that letter **D** is the **Δ** or uppercase Delta symbol which can also be the symbol for Doorway. It was originally derived from the Phoenician letter daleth and the D was drawn as a door or gate. Likewise, at some vault sites, when you are very close to an entrance you may come across the **D, Δ** or even a lowercase delta symbol.

Remkes

116

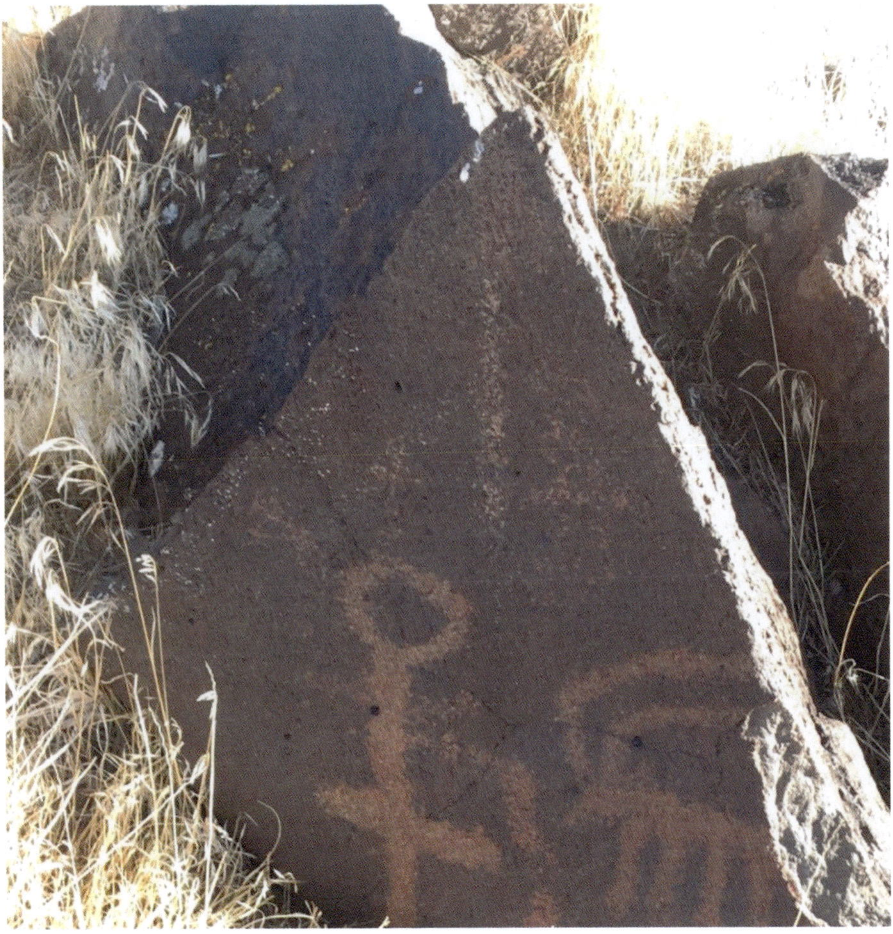

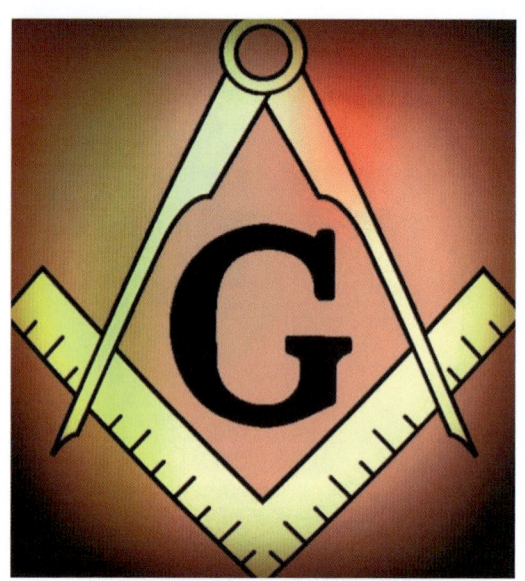

The Compass (or Compasses) and Square
Notice the G in the middle

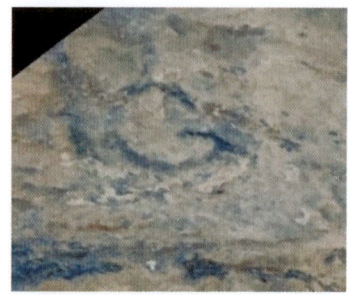

I believe this G has multiple layers of meaning as do most symbols. Some of the possible meanings could be:
Gnosis
Genesis
Generation
Genius
God
Geometry
Gold
The number 7

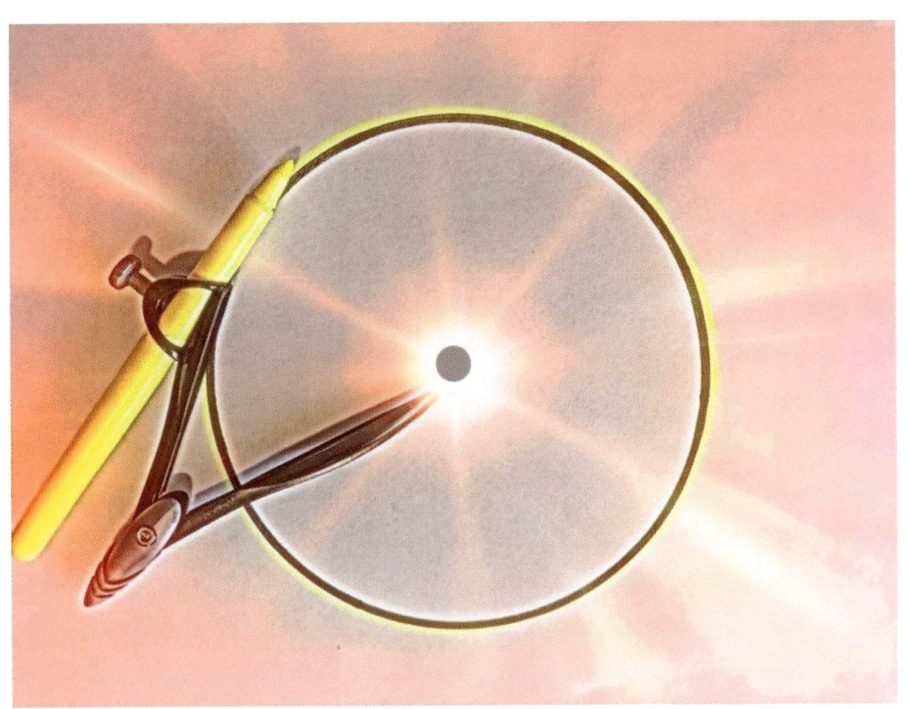

A Compass

A compass, like the compass used in Masonry, is an instrument used to draw circles or the parts of circles called arcs.
This also can be used for taking or marking off distances along a line. It has two movable arms which are hooked together where one arm has a pointed end and the other arm holds a pencil or pen. This type of compass is also called a pair of compasses.

A Compass

Another type of compass is described in Wikipidia: A compass is an instrument used for navigation and direction relative to the geographic cardinal directions (or points). Usually, a diagram called a compass rose shows the directions north, south, east, and west on the compass face as abbreviated initials. When the compass is used, the rose can be aligned with the corresponding geographic directions; for example, the "N" mark on the rose points northward. Compasses often display markings for angles in degrees in addition to (or sometimes instead of) the rose. North corresponds to 0°, and the angles increase clockwise, so east is 90° degrees, south is 180°, and west is 270°. These numbers allow the compass to show magnetic north or true North azimuths or bearings, which are commonly stated in this notation. If magnetic declination between the magnetic North and true North at latitude angle and longitude angle is known, then direction of magnetic North also gives direction of true North.

The Seal of Solomon (Star of David) is made of opposites.

I believe this is a symbol similar in meaning to the compass and square, as it appears to be opposites. The moon symbol on the top, and the sun on the bottom.

I believe information found at some of these sites references Adam and Eve, the Garden of Eden and DNA.

My Key E DNA

When I researched the name Edna, I found these pieces of information:
Meaning: "delight" (see Eden).

From Hebrew עֶדְנָה ("pleasure; delight"); a variant of Eden in the Book of Tobit.

--Derived from the same word as the biblical Garden of Eden.

At many of the sites, names and dates that just appear to be "graffiti" are pieces of information. The name "Edna" has been at many of the sites that I have studied. One remote site, had a man's name with the + like this as well. I found three places it had been done and all three were very discreet and heavily coded. And after studying the man's name, I do not think he was ever married to anyone by the name of Edna, unless he was having an affair.

The name "Michael" was the name of Adam before (and after) he came to mortality. God passed to him certain keys. He will be the one sounding the trumpet heralding the resurrection of the dead.

After studying the rest of the information at some of these sites, it seems to be referring to the garden of Eden and to DNA. I was astounded the first time I discovered this.

"E" in EDNA, I believe could be "East" and then "DNA" In Genesis 3:24 it says:
"So he drove out the man; and he placed at the east of the garden of Eden Cherubims, and a flaming sword which turned every way, to keep the way of the tree of life."
The sun also rises in the East.

From what I am understanding from studying multiple sites, I believe they are telling us that something happend with our DNA when Adam and Eve partook of the tree of knowledge of good and evil, which created the ability to die physically. Adam and Eve seemed to have known this consequence and willingly chose to take of the fruit so that they could have children and obey all of God's commandments.

The serpent, to me, appears to be DNA itself. At least in one sense of the meaning.

Christ prepared a way before the foundation of the world for us to live again both physically and spiritually, after we were cut off from the presence of God. He is our connection with Heaven while on this earth and is our Mediator. He overcame the serpent, of death and hell and of the grave. The serpent was raised. He is the only way to life.

After researching more, I came to understand that memory is locked up in our DNA.

Gnostic Warrior said: "Simply put, your DNA holds your future, your past and the lost keys to your ancestors' ancient history." I wonder if this is why there is such obsession with grail bloodlines. I wonder if since memory is in our DNA, if this key helps unlock the secrets at many of these ancient sites. I wonder if my ancestors' involvement with some of these things led me to the path that I am on now, although I was never personally taught to see what is hidden at these locations. I do know that the burning in my heart when I read my ancestors' words in family history, led me to look for our family's lost mines. And with what I saw while on this quest, I gained a desire to understand more of what I am seeing in these environments.

Photo courtesy of Chris Hegg

Notice the tail bone, the snake, the ladder, & the circumpuncts etc...
A human DNA strand has 33 complete turns and a spine has 33 vertabrae.

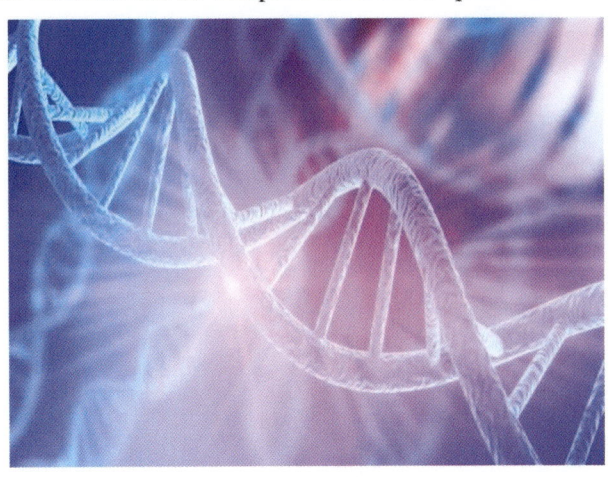

A 33 degree Mason is the top degree in Scottish Right Freemasonry.
**Notice the spiral ladder in the DNA strand.
I believe Jacob's Ladder in the Bible symbolizes the bridge between heaven and earth.**

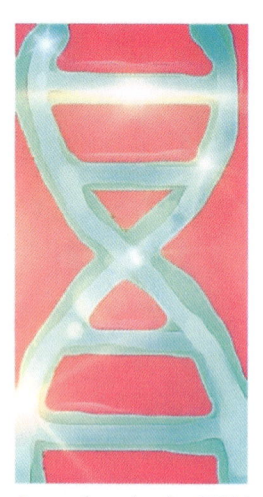

Notice the hourglass in the DNA strand.

Caduceus
(Frohan Froben)

Notice the ladders, and the wagon axle etc...

Notice the top of the image, similar to a heart, looks like the top of the caduceus.

I believe these symbolize tongs, and multiple other things, but could they also be depicting chromosomes?
At this particular site I believe there could be a possibility.

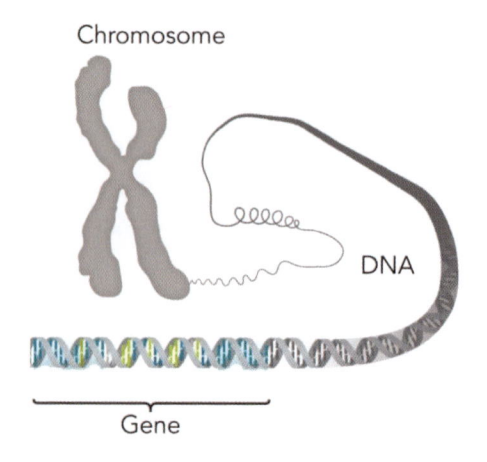

129

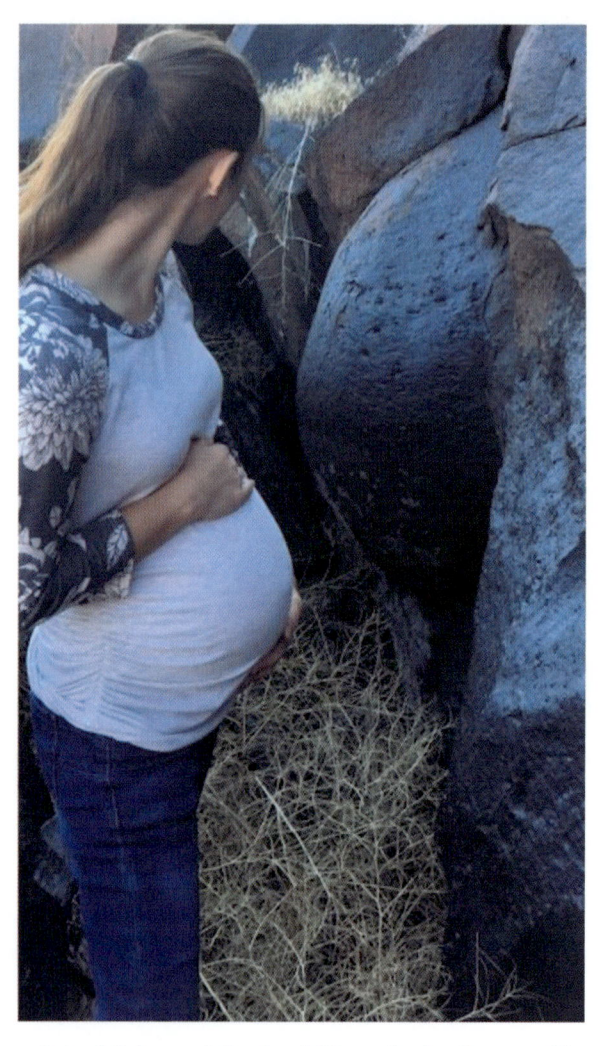

One view point of this rock looked like a baby bump. From another view, it appeared to be a dragon waiting for a baby to be born. (Pictured on next page. Also, notice the symbol that looks to be symbolic of ovaries.

The theme at this site and the story of the Red Dragon reminds me of what is written in Revelation 12 of the Bible concerning Christ overcoming Satan and death. The theme seemed to also focus a lot on DNA and the Garden of Eden and Eve.

Remkes

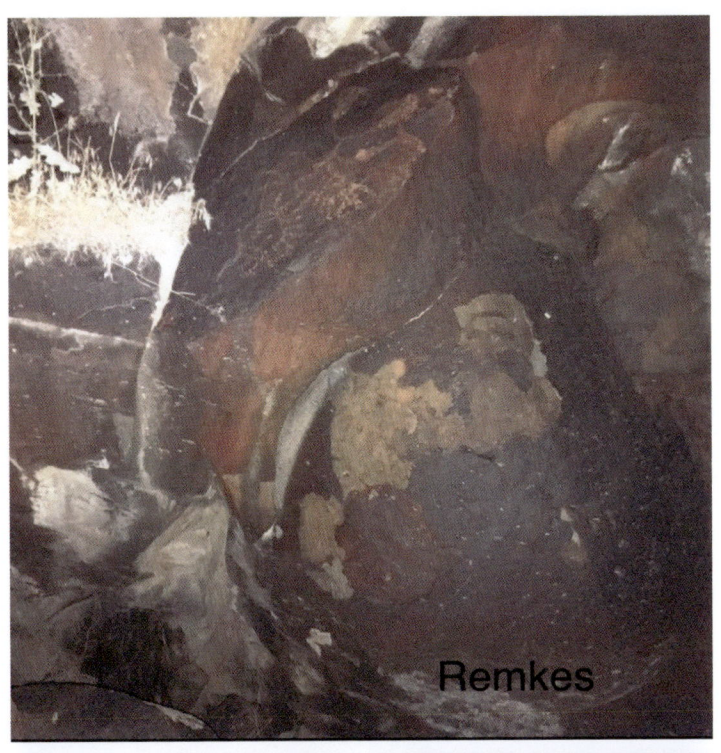

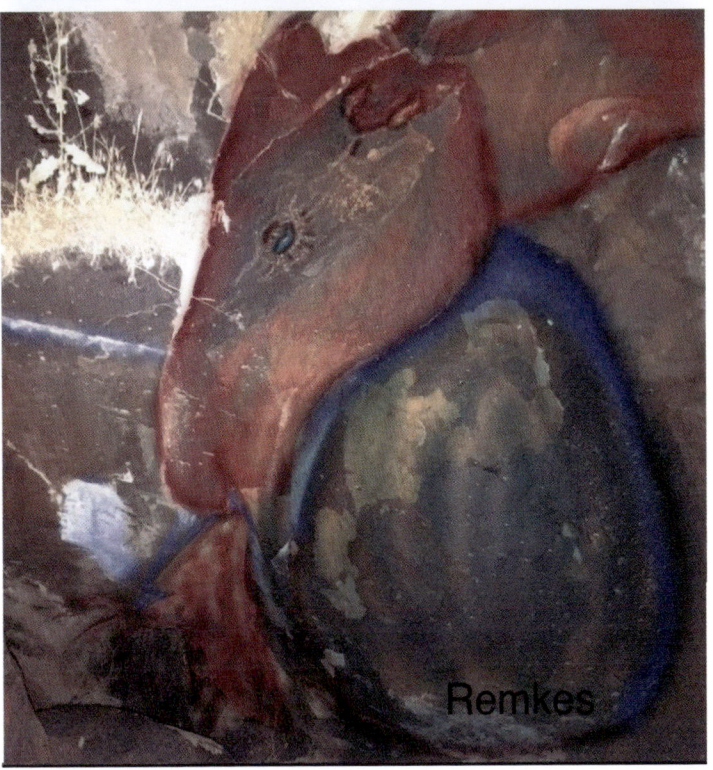

Remkes

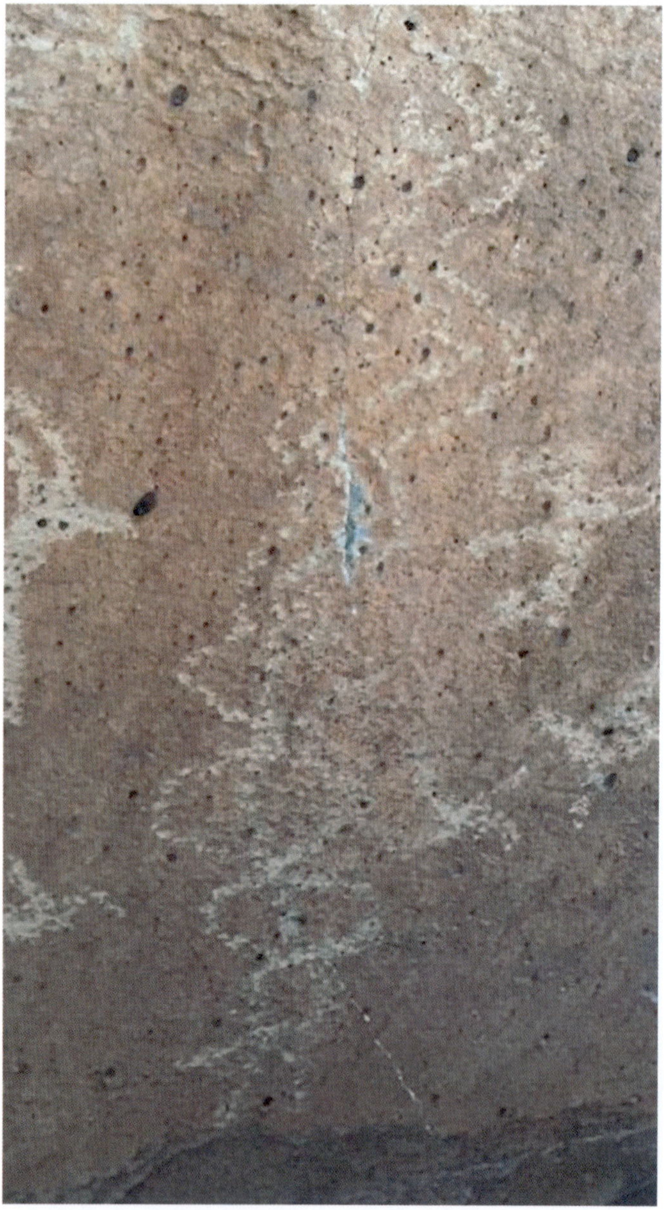

According to some sources, some cache sites are set up like a clock. Some map types will also tell you which way to read the clock. Cartographers were said to have set up some of these sites in various ways. Sometimes, there will be multiple caches at one site and you need to find the locations on the outer part while some sites may have the cache at the center point. Or there may be several central points for multiple caches. It appears many of these sites use various markers and landmarks to help align towards an invisible point where all of the lines cross marking a cache or mine.

Some things to think about:

There are 12 numbers surrounding the center of the clock, and the center would be the 13. Same as with Christ's 12 apostles, He is the center and is the 13.

Christ is said to have come in the Meridian of times. The etymology for Meridian goes back to the Latin word "meridianum" or the word "noon." This comes from "medius" which means "middle" and "dies" for "day." I also believe that He is said to have come during the Meridian of times, because in the Eternal perspective, we have the Pre-existence, Mortal Life, and The After-life. Christ came during the Mortal time which is in the middle of the three. It is important to know about the other two perspectives in order to understand the big picture.

Writing found in an old beehive kiln. I suspect this is part of a written map marking someting hidden by the Knights of the Golden Circle or another similar society.

**The circumpunct is the eye of
a hidden owl.**

Often I have found the circumpunct hidden in the landscape.
Sometimes, they will be huge geoglyphs.
Often they will be smaller and will resemble a firepit.

Notice this circumpunct is an eye on a rock face. Notice the man's headpiece and the broken area on the rock is triangular.

138

139

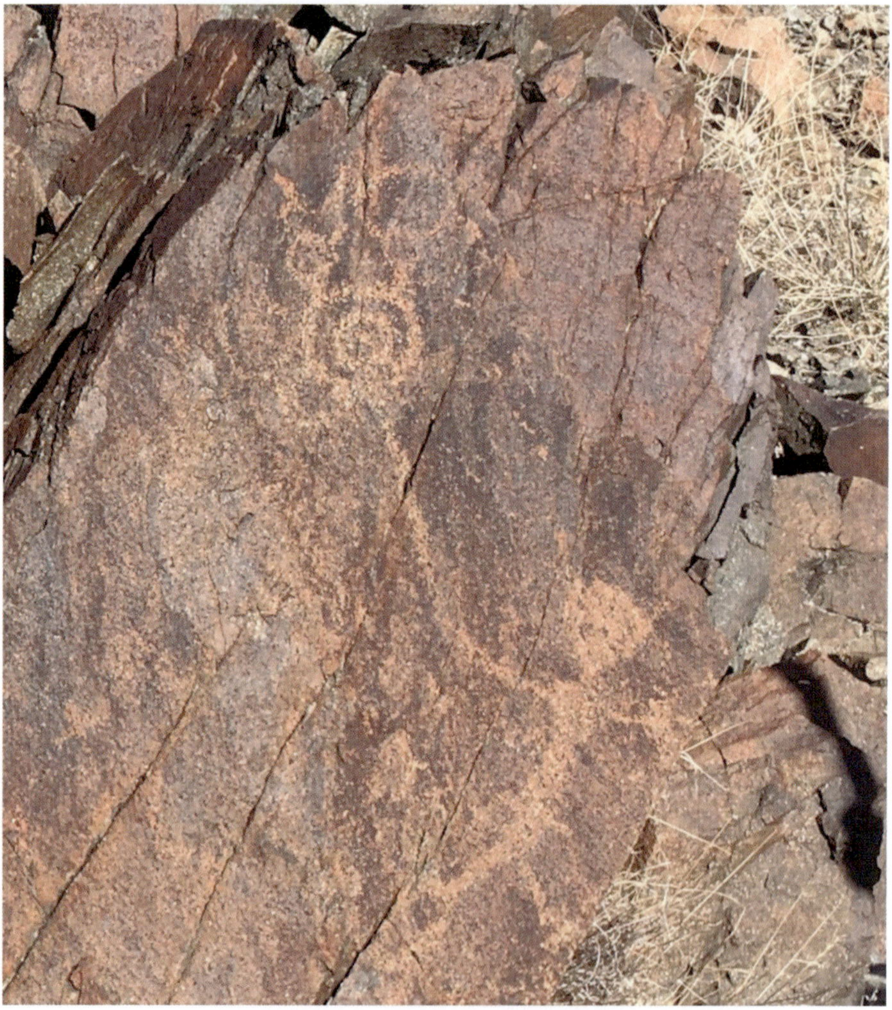

Notice the head of what looks to be perhaps a badger.

Notice the circumpunct is the eye of what looks to be the head of a goose. Birds are often directionals, and I would investigate the place where this goose is looking.

142

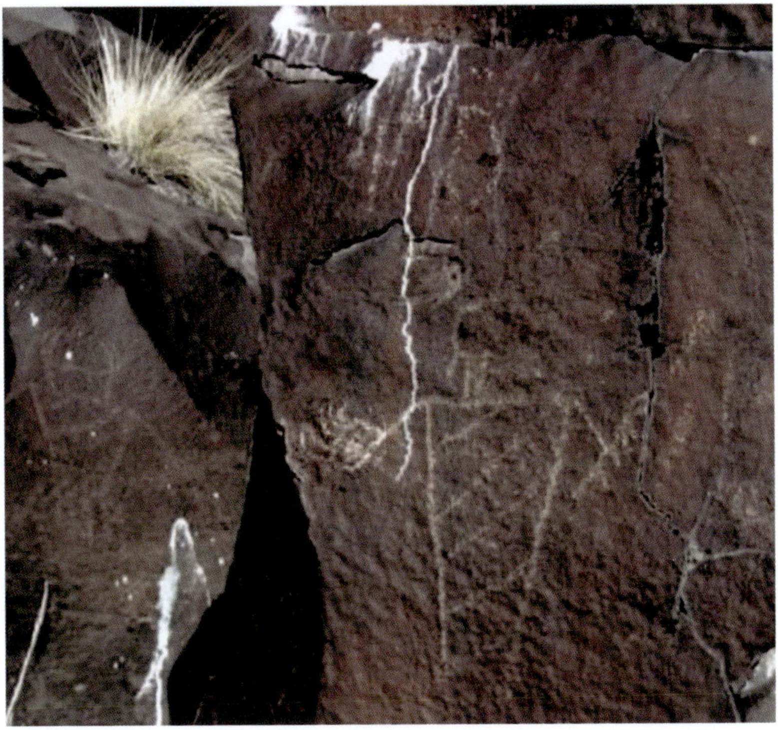

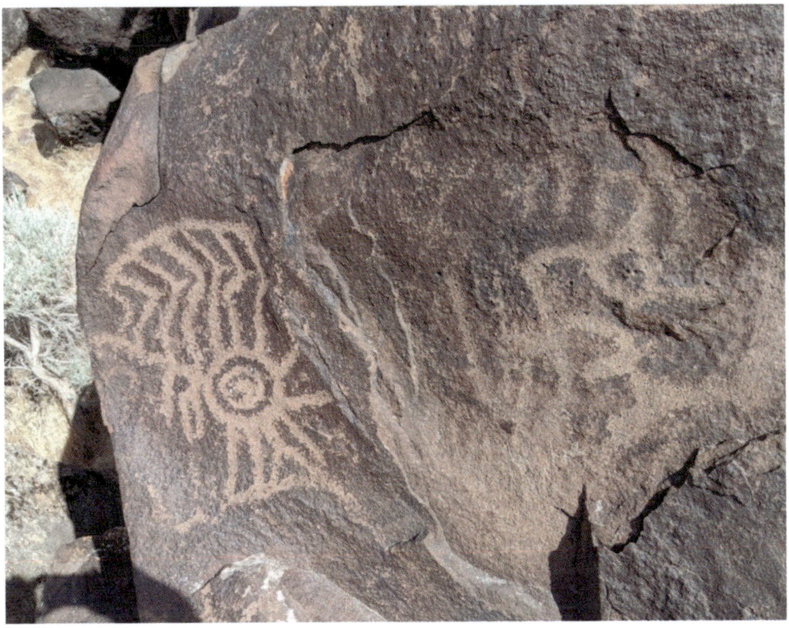

Hidden Crocodile at beginning of an important site

      Crocodiles can be symbols of wisdom and the protector and keeper of all knowledge. They can symbolize sovereignty. In Egypt, the crocodile was often associated with the god "Sobek." Sobek was one of the oldest dieties mentioned in the Pyramid Texts as a funerary god. Sobek's father was said to have been Set (or Seth). He was known as "Lord of the waters" and was said to have risen from the primeval waters to create the world. The Coffin Texts, (the funerary texts) used during the Middle Kingdon has Sobek labled as, "He who rises in the east and sets in the west.

Notice the circumpunct is the eye of the crocodile.

Crocodiles can often be associated with death traps as crocodiles are quick to rise from the mud and snap at their victim killing them quickly and usually without warning.

Notice the incorporated usage of the holes.

146

When I first started studying cache sites, I knew that I needed to think like those who set them up. After years, of studying, I am still fascinated by all of the information that can be packed into their messages.

Here is an example of what I am seeing hidden in this one word. I like to explore all of the ideas that I see.

Notice how the A's look like the compass and square. When I see this, it often means the person who wrote the symbol also conceled a message. It makes me aware that I need to look at the message in as many angles and ways as I can. I like to look at things from as many perspectives as possible. Often there will be anagrams.

Here, P MALAM spells PM at the begining and AM at the end.

(TIME and the Clock are important ties to many sites.) PM is an abbreviation for the Latin phrase Post Meridiem, meaning "after midday". And AM is for "ante meridiem" meaning before midday.

Also notice that MALAM is a palindrome. A palindrome is a word that is the same spelled frontwards and backwards. The meaning of the ouroboros and palindrome are similar as is I AM the begining and the end. Notice "MALAM" also looks like the I AM spelled both ways. Also, the world MAL is usually associated with bad and with the reversed meaning of the MAL would be good. So this has the opposing meanings here.

The story of Moses and the burning bush comes to my mind when I look at the possible meanings of the word I AM. The way God introduced Himself to Moses. And Moses replied to God "Here Am I."

I find it interesting that God introduced Himself to Moses as "I AM that I AM."

Now Moses kept the flock of Jethro his father in law, the priest of Midian: and he led the flock to the backside of the desert, and came to the mountain of God, even to Horeb.

2 And the angel of the LORD appeared unto him in a flame of fire out of the midst of a bush: and he looked, and, behold, **the bush burned with fire, and the bush was not consumed.**

3 And Moses said, I wiill now turn aside, and see this great sight, why the bush is not burnt.

4 And when the LORD saw that he turned aside to see, God called unto him out of the midst of the bush, and said, Moses, Moses. And he said, **Here am I.**

5 And he said, Draw not nigh hither: put off thy shoes from off thy feet, for the place whereon thou standest is holy ground.

6 Moreover he said, I am the God of thy father, the God of Abraham, the God of Isaac, and the God of Jacob. And Moses hid his face; for he was afraid to look upon God.

7 And the LORD said, I have surely seen the affliction of my people which are in Egypt, and have heard their cry by reason of their taskmasters; for I know their sorrows;

8 And I am come down to deliver them out of the hand of the Egyptians, and to bring them up out of that land unto a good land and a large, unto a land flowing with milk and honey; unto the place of the Canaanites, and the Hittites, and the Amorites, and the Perizzites, and the Hivites, and the Jebusites.

9 Now therefore, behold, the cry of the children of Israel is come unto me: and I have also seen the oppression wherewith the Egyptians oppress them.

10 Come now therefore, and I will send thee unto Pharaoh, that thou mayest bring forth my people the children of Israel out of Egypt.

11 And Moses said unto God, **Who am I**, that I should go unto Pharaoh, and that I should bring forth the children of Israel out of Egypt?

12 And he said, Certainly I will be with thee; and this shall be a token unto thee, that I have sent thee: When thou hast brought forth the people out of Egypt, ye shall serve God upon this mountain.

13 And Moses said unto God, Behold, when I come unto the children of Israel, and shall say unto them, The God of your fathers hath sent me unto you; and they shall say to me, What is his name? what shall I say unto them?

14 And God said unto Moses, **I AM THAT I AM**: and he said, Thus shalt thou say unto the children of Israel, **I AM** hath sent me unto you.

15 And God said moreover unto Moses, Thus shalt thou say unto the children of Israel, the LORD God of your fathers, the God of Abraham, the God of Isaac, and the God of Jacob, hath sent me unto you: this is my name for ever, and this is my memorial unto all generations

THE BURNING BUSH
(Painting by Stefan Duncan)
Another example of gold in the refiner's fire.

I also found it interesting that the word "Moses" in Hebrew is "Mosheh" which is spelled with Mem-Shin-Heh which is 345 in Gemetria and the way God introduced himself to Moses as "I AM" or Eheyeh Asher Eheyeh. This would be a palindrome in Gemetria! 543, which seems to show that Moses is a reflection of Yaweh 345. The phrase, "As Above, So Below" may be found here as well.

The word Malam or Malum in Latin can mean evil, or apple. Which makes me think of the fruit Adam and Eve partook of in the Garden of Eden.

In India, Maal-amm means, "One who has the knowledge of Directions."

When I look at this coded message, I also see the word PMAL as the word LAMP when read in reverse. The word lamp is associated with light and the etymoligcal word goes back to the word Torch.

I am also seeing the word MAP hidden in the P MALAM as well. The way they made the P is also an R as there is a lower part to it, but it is fainter. So this would likely be an anagram for RAM on the left side of the L. RAM is often for "Royal Arch Mason." There is also a ram's head hidden in the scenery that I believe represents Amun Ra. Also, I believe the association with Amun Ra is why they use the ram symbol on may petroglyphs with information added into the way they drew these symbols.

 I believe the person who wrote this had family ties to Ireland. And there is an extra meaning for the word "lám" as this means "hand" or "palm of the hand" in old Irish. (*The Red Hand of Ulster* may be good refrence to one of the meanings behind the red hand found at some sites.)

A.L. –*Anno Lucis*, "In the Year of light" the date used by Ancient Craft Masons.

P.M.- Past Master

A.M. –*Anno Mundi*, "In The Year of the World". The date used in the Ancient and Accepted Scottish Rite

R. A.M. – Royal Arch Mason

In Hebrew the preposition מעל (*ma'al*), means upward, on top of, or above. The verb עלה (*'ala*), means to go up or ascend

I am sure there is more information hidden here as well.

A symbol of the Axis Mundi

2 Nephi 2:8 (from the Book of Mormon)
Wherefore, how great the importance to make these things known unto the inhabitants of the earth, that they may know that there is no flesh that can dwell in the presence of God, save it be through the merits, and mercy, and grace of the Holy Messiah, who layeth down his life according to the flesh, and taketh it again by the power of the Spirit, that he may bring to pass the ressurection of the dead, being the first that should rise.

2 Nephi 2:11

For it must needs be, that there is an opposition in all things. If not so, my firstborn in the wilderness, righteousness could not be brought to pass, neither wickedness, neither holiness nor misery, neither good nor bad. Wherefore, all things must needs be a compound in one; wherefore, if it should be one body it must needs remain as dead, having no life neither death, nor corruption nor incorruption, happiness nor misery, neither sense nor insensibility.

2 Nephi 2:24-25

But behold, all things have been done in the wisdom of him who knoweth all things.

Adam *fell* that men might be; and me are, that they might have joy. And the Messiah cometh in the fulness of time, that he may redeem the children of men from the fall. And because that they are redeemed from the fall they have become free forever, knowing good from evil; to act for themselves and not to be acted upon, save it be by the punishment of the law at the great and last day, according to the commandments which God hath given.
Wherefore, men are free according to the flesh; an*d* all hings are given them which are expedient unto man. And they are free to choose liberty and eternal life, through the great Mediator of all men, or to choose captivity and death, according to the captivity and power of the devil; for he seeketh that all men might be *miserable* like unto himself.

The empty tomb
(Unknown photo credit, edited.)
The Resurrection is the rising of the Son.
Just as each new day, we look to the East for the rising of the sun.

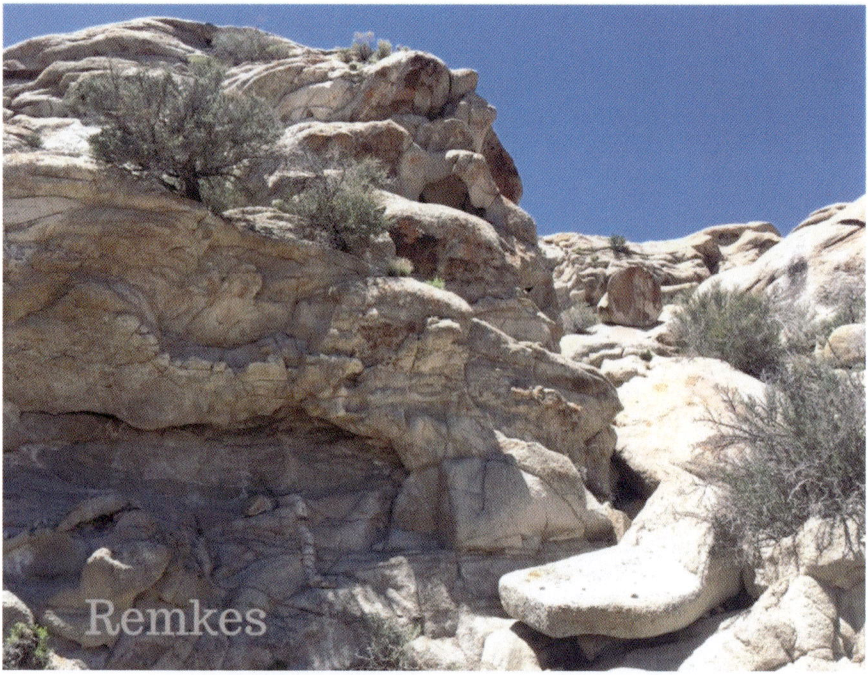
Remkes

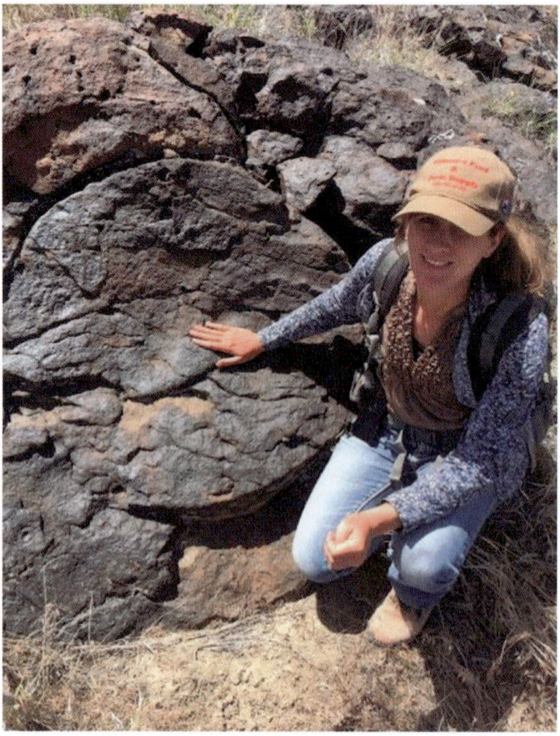

157

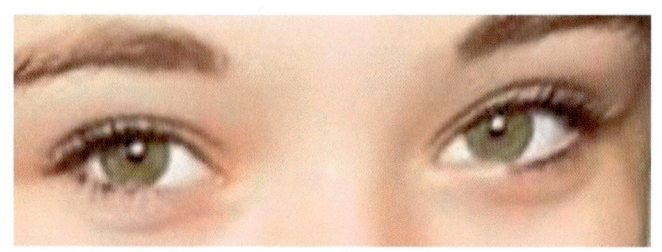

The light of the body is the eye

The light of the body is the eye: if therefore thine eye be single, thy whole body shall be full of light. But if thine eye be evil, thy whole body shall be full of darkness. If therefore the light that is in thee be darkness, how great is that darkness! **Matthew 6:22-23**

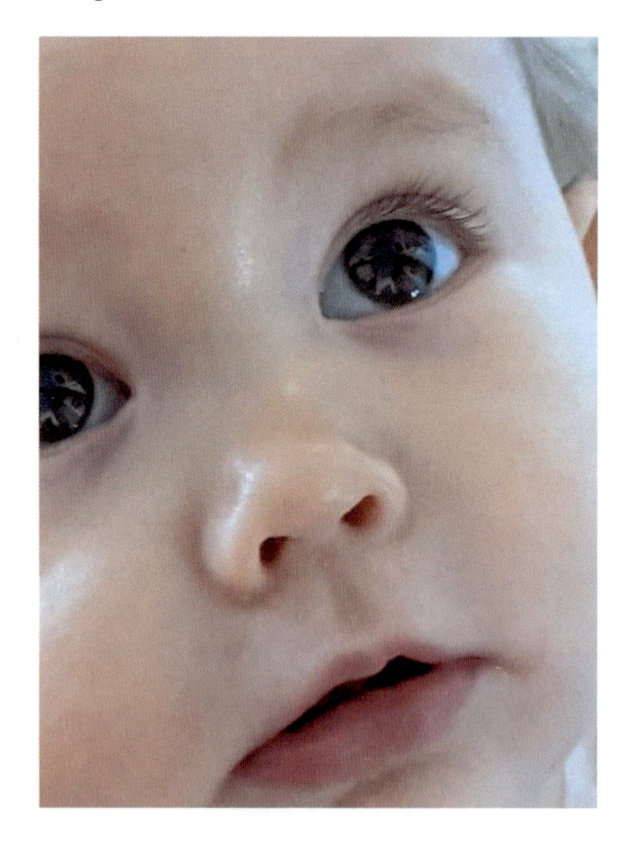

The Kingdom of God is within you.- Luke 17:21

'Man shall not live by bread alone, but by every word that proceedeth out of the mouth of God." Matthew 4:4

159

ΑΩ

"I am Alpha and Omega, the beginning and the end, the first and the last. Blessed are they that do his commandments, that they may have right to the tree of life." Revelation 22:13-14

Jesus Christ is the Light, the Life and the Hope of the world. It is only through Him that we are saved.

The circumpunct can be a reminder that we should strive to be like the SON of God. We should always be giving and full of light. We have been given a reminder of the Son with the rising and the setting of the sun with each passing day.

> "And the light shineth in darkness; and the darkness comprehended it not." John 1:5

God did not create evil.
Just as darkness is the absence of light, evil is the absence of God.

(Attr. Albert Einstein)

Printed in Great Britain
by Amazon